Hey, God,
Why Is It
Taking So Long?

Navigating Through Life One Step at a Time

Lynette Hagin

Hey, God,

Why Is It Taking So Long?

Navigating Through Life One Step at a Time

Lynette Hagin

Unless otherwise indicated, all Scripture quotations in this volume are from the *King James Version* of the Bible.

Scripture quotations marked AMPLIFIED are taken from *The Amplified Bible*, Old Testament copyright © 1965, 1987 by the Zondervan Corporation. The Amplified New Testament copyright © 1954, 1958, 1987 by The Lockman Foundation. Used by permission.

Scripture quotations marked *NIV* are taken from the *Holy Bible, New International Version®*. *NIV®*. Copyright © 1973, 1978, 1984 by International Bible Society. Used by permission of Zondervan. All rights reserved.

First Printing 2004

ISBN 0-89276-800-2

In the U.S. write:
Kenneth Hagin Ministries
P.O. Box 50126
Tulsa, OK 74150-0126
1-888-28-FAITH
www.rhema.org

In Canada write:
Kenneth Hagin Ministries
P.O. Box 335, Station D
Etobicoke (Toronto), Ontario
Canada, M9A 4X3

CONTENTS

PREFACE vii

1. Waiting and Wondering 1

2. Successfully Handling the Seasons of Life 17

3. Commit, Prepare, Wait, Prove 37

4. Thank God for the Holy Ghost! 69

5. 'I Am Determined!' 89

6. You Can Totally Rely on God 111

7. Casting Your Cares 139

8. Peace in Troubled Times 155

9. How to Receive and Fulfill God's Plan 181

10. Finding My Place Through Prayer 203

11. Staying the Course 217

12. Turning Stumbling Blocks
    Into Stepping-Stones 235

13. Commitment Plus Contentment
    Equals Joy 249

14. The Blessings of Waiting Upon the Lord 277

15. For Such a Time as This 301

My love for the Lord became apparent at the age of two. Although I do not remember this incident, my mother relayed to me that at the age of two, she found me in her bedroom. I had gotten in her closet and put on her high heel shoes, found a handkerchief, and was kneeling by her bed crying. Startled at my actions, she soon realized that I was mimicking what I had seen at church. Often, the church members would be gathered around the altar with a handkerchief and crying out to God. My heart was sensitive to the things of God at that young age. I do remember joining the adults around the altar at the age of four. I would pray fervently as they did.

I remember well that much of my praying had to do with praying out the plan of God for my life. I always wanted to be in His divine will. I'm so thankful for my godly parents who taught me the importance of placing God first in my life. I knew better than to question if we were going to church or not at the designated times. It was not a matter of "if" we were going, but the question was, "When are we going to leave?" I was at church more than I was at home. But the love for God that was instilled in my heart by being continually in church is something that I'll always be thankful for.

This book has been a dream that I was not sure I wanted to share with the world. I really am a very private person. My relationship with God has been a very private adventure and for many years, I wanted to keep it that way. When God began to nudge me with the idea that He wanted me to share my experiences with others, I was quite hesitant at first. They were so sacred to me that I wanted to keep them between just God and me.

However, in His gentle way, the Lord assured me that sharing my experiences would encourage others to follow God's plan for their life. I trust this book does that for you. The lessons in this book were not received from someone I read after, but life lessons of my own. The Lord has been my Best Friend. I hope that He will become your Best Friend as well.

I want to say "thank-you" to my dad, the late Vernon Tipton, and to my mother, Mrs. Mary Tipton, who taught me to love God with all my heart. Their untiring example of loving and serving people has been a wonderful example for me to follow. Always believing in me, they taught me that with God by my side, I could do anything. In the last several years before his homegoing, my dad would say, "Honey, you need to preach more." Daddy, I trust that you are watching from the grandstands. The preach comes on me quite frequently now. My dad always encouraged women preachers, even when most thought that a woman's place was not in the pulpit.

A great big thanks to my loving husband, Ken, who has always told me that I was the "love" of his life. He's been there to encourage me when my knees were shaking at the thoughts of public speaking. One time I was so frightened that I became deathly ill. He had to pray for my body to be well. He kissed me and said, "I don't know why you're frightened; you're a terrific speaker." Thank you, honey. I love you very much.

I want to say "thank-you" to my two children, Craig and Denise, who have always so understood when ministry would get a little hectic in their young years. Ministry truly became their life as well. They often had to sleep in restaurants in a nearby booth while my husband and I were fellowshipping with and ministering to others. Thank you, kids, for never becoming bitter over ministry, but for being there for your dad and me.

Hey, God, Why Is It Taking So Long?

I want to say "thank-you" to my father-in-law, the late Kenneth E. Hagin, and my mother-in-law, Mrs. Oretha Hagin, for being a wonderful example for my husband. He was taught well to honor and care for a wife. The flowers that I always receive on special occasions from my husband are a result of your example. I am grateful for the revelation of the principles of faith that were taught by my father-in-law. The truths that I received from his teachings have helped me to courageously carry out the plan of God for my life.

Lastly, let me say as you read this book, I trust that you will allow the Holy Spirit to speak to your heart. God loves you very much. He has special plans for your life. Dare to trust Him and step out on His promises. As you do, He will always be there for you. It may seem like a long time before your dreams become realities but remember—God will lead you down His chosen path, one step at a time.

Lynette Hagin

CHAPTER 1

Waiting and Wondering

Raised in a pastor's home, I grew up around various aspects of the ministry and always saw ministry as a way of life. From very early on, I knew ministry was my calling. I knew I wanted to spend my time helping people. I knew I would one day marry a preacher. And I thought I knew just how each part of this plan would come to pass.

Well, I was wrong about how the plan would come to pass! I came to discover that the Bible is indeed true—God's thoughts are not my thoughts (Isa. 55:8)! And God's plan was not my plan. Yes, ministry is my calling. And yes, I have spent the better part of my life helping people. I even married a preacher (Kenneth Hagin Jr.). But there was a time in my life when I didn't know how any of this was ever going to happen.

Hey, God, Why Is It Taking So Long?

When I was 29 years old, Ken and I had been married 9 years. Together, we were active in the ministry, helping his father, Kenneth E. Hagin, and helping people.

Then came a time when I was no longer in the ministry. My husband was still in the ministry; he was busy starting RHEMA Bible Training Center. But I was a mother with two young children who needed a lot of my attention. My place in ministry seemed to have disappeared.

I couldn't help thinking, *"What about my calling to the ministry? What about my helping people? What about God's plan for my life?"*

Then I began wondering, *What* is *God's plan for my life?* For the first time, I wasn't active in ministry. What was going on? Was I to remain quietly on the sidelines while my husband moved on in ministry?

Sometimes it's difficult to find your place in the world. Everybody thinks they know what you're supposed to do with your life and they feel free to share their opinions. But in our heart, we hold dreams of what we want to be, and we hear the divine calling of God's plan for our life.

As you face your daily to-do list, God's plan for your life may seem far away. At times, you may even wonder whether you only *imagined* those things He spoke to your heart. And at times, you may look around and see other people (even those you love) move ahead with their plans and wonder why it's taking so long for God to reveal the next step in His plan for you.

But God's timing is perfect. He knows the secrets in your heart and the dreams He gave you—dreams He still plans to make come true. God loves you; you matter to Him! And He is actively working on your behalf to fashion you according to His plan for your life—the plan He destined for you before time began.

If you are wondering what you're supposed to do in the meantime—while you're waiting for what God spoke to come to pass—you are not alone. In this book, I will share with you the valuable lessons I learned during those hard times of waiting and wondering when God's plan for my life would finally come to pass. I pray that my experiences will help you stand strong and remain hopeful during your season of waiting.

Holding On to God's Promises

In 1974, I had prayed desperately and earnestly, "God, what would You have for my life? What would you have me to do?" It was a point in my life when I desperately needed to know what God had planned for me.

Hey, God, Why Is It Taking So Long?

Until that time, I had always been involved in some aspect of ministry. As I said, I was raised in a pastor's home and had always been involved in doing many things for the Lord. But in 1974, at the time when I began to seek God for His plan for *me*, my place in ministry had seemed to disappear. My children were young. RHEMA Bible Training Center had just started, and my husband was quite busy taking care of the school.

This season of my life was a real quiet time of ministry for me. It seemed that my only involvement in ministry was through prayer. Praying was all I could do at that time. So I began praying, "Lord, what do You have planned for me?"

As I prayed day after day after day, the Lord began to drop some things in my heart. And when I was 29 years old, one of the things He revealed to me was that I would someday host a conference for women. He did not tell me when. He told me that He would let me know when the time was right, saying, "I'll let you know when the time comes that these things I have told you will be fulfilled, and you will walk out My plan one step at a time."

More than 25 years later, in January 2001, as I was praying, the Lord let me know, "Now! Now is the time!" The first annual *Kindle the Flame* Women's Conference, held September 27–29, 2001, fulfilled one of the dreams the Lord put in my heart so long ago—the dream to ignite the spark of divine purpose within each woman so she could return to her family and job with fresh enthusiasm.

Each September, women from across the nation and the world gather on the RHEMA campus for the event that has become one of my greatest joys. Hosting a national women's conference wasn't always a joy. I can remember when God's call to hold meetings for women was one of my greatest apprehensions!

When the Lord first spoke to me during that time of prayer and let me know He wanted me to hold women's meetings, I didn't want to do it. I had seen too many women's groups get off-base doctrinally and become "hyper-spiritual," neglecting their homes and families.

For many years, I wrestled with the Lord's instructions. But I didn't just sit on my hands in the meantime. Since that time in 1974, the Lord kept me busy with many other things in the ministry, such as general manager for all the Kenneth Hagin Ministries offices, director of RHEMA Bible Training Center, and carrying out all the normal duties of the pastor's wife of a church of over 8,000 members! But every time I began to pray out the steps of my life and ministry, I always ended up praying about ministering to women!

Hey, God, Why Is It Taking So Long?

I agonized about it, saying, "Lord, please, not me. I don't want to do that. I'm happy doing what I'm doing right now in the ministry. I really don't need anything else to do!" Of course, I finally yielded and said, "Okay, I'll do it. But You will have to show me the plan. You will have to show me what I'm to do." And He said, "I'll do that."

Over the years, I protected the dream God had given me, hiding His instructions in my heart. In my mind, I figured the plan would take shape when I turned 40. Forty came and went, and the Lord didn't say, "Go ye!" Then 50 came and went, and there was still no "Go ye." I thought, *God, this is wonderful! Maybe You were only testing my willingness to obey You.*

But in the year 2001, the Lord said, "Now is the time!" And I said, "Okay, then You have to give me the plan." You see, although God had told me that one of my callings would be ministering to women, He had not given me the specific plan to fulfill that call.

It was then that He said He would gather an army of women around me. The United States Army has always been close to my heart because my husband served in that branch of the military, and he still loves the Army. I thought, *Yes, Lord, I know how to lead an army of women. If that's what You want me to do, I can do it!*

God showed me that the army of women would need to know how to balance being a godly woman, wife, and mother and that they would need to know how to balance their divine calling with all that these roles entailed. These women would be called—even as Queen Esther was called—*for such a time as this* (Esther 4:14).

All those years, I kept in my heart the plan that God had given me. Even when it seemed in the natural that things weren't happening, I held on to His promises. During the years when I was focused on raising my children and supporting my husband's ministry (those years when I wasn't active in ministry and was nowhere close to holding annual women's conferences), I held on to God's plan for my life. I prayed about it, protected the dreams, and waited for just the right time—God's time!

As you can imagine, the first night of the first *Kindle the Flame* Women's Conference in 2001 was a special night for me. I was able to witness the Lord bringing to pass something He had placed in my heart 25 years earlier.

Now, through the *Kindle the Flame* Women's Conferences, my goal is to help other women fulfill the plan that God has given them. But my heart goes out to *anyone* who has a dream that God gave him . . . but feels he is miles away from seeing that dream come true.

Perhaps you have held something in your heart for many years, and you have wondered, *God, when will Your plan for my life come to pass?* The Lord is saying that He has kept you for such a time as this! Each one of us may have already accomplished something for God, but God has a special purpose for us at this time and in this hour!

Each and every one of us is called. And if you feel unqualified, I want to encourage you. God doesn't call the qualified. He *qualifies* the *called*! And if you will totally rely on the Lord your God, you will accomplish what He has called you to do.

For good reason, the Scripture passage we chose for the *Kindle the Flame* conference is Psalm 18:28 and 29 from the *New International Version*. It says, "You, O Lord, keep my lamp burning; my God turns my darkness into light. With your help I can advance against a troop; with my God I can scale a wall."

It doesn't matter how tall the wall is that blocks the path God has called you to walk. With God, you are able to overcome it!

Faith in the Power of God

Once the time was right, I remember how quickly the Lord put that first conference together. He told me who to invite to speak at the meetings, and each of the three women was available for the precise dates God had put on my heart. Usually these women book their schedules a year in advance, but all three were willing and able to speak at that first conference in 2001. I knew the Lord had put it all together.

But little did I know what would be occurring in the United States of America at the time of our first *Kindle the Flame* conference. The date for that first conference was right after the horrific September 11 terrorist attacks on our nation. When God said, "Now is the time; this is to be the date; these are to be the speakers," little did I know the condition our nation would be in. But God knew; He is never surprised or caught off guard.

God's plan for my life began to unfold in an important hour. I knew I was living in an important time and, even now, these days in which we live are vitally important. Yet we are not without support, as we can see from the words of the Apostle Paul.

1 CORINTHIANS 2:1–5,9

1   And I, brethren, when I came to you, came not with excellency of speech or of wisdom, declaring unto you the testimony of God.

2   For I determined not to know any thing among you, save Jesus Christ, and him crucified.

3   And I was with you in weakness, and in fear, and in much trembling.

4   And my speech and my preaching was not with enticing words of man's wisdom, but in demonstration of the Spirit and of power:

5   That your faith should not stand in the wisdom of men, but in the power of God. . . .

9   But as it is written, Eye hath not seen, nor ear heard, neither have entered into the heart of man, the things which God hath prepared for them that love him.

I don't want your faith to rest in my words or my wisdom—or in the words of *any* man or woman—but in God and in His mighty power.

I marvel at some people's mastery of the English language. Some people can give eloquent messages that just seem to flow effortlessly. Some people have a gift to speak so beautifully. I haven't been endowed with that gift. Whenever I speak, I just deliver my heart. Whether or not my words come out eloquently doesn't matter to me. The most important thing is that your heart be touched and that you be changed by God's power and might.

You Are God's Masterpiece

God has a plan and a purpose for your life. His Word proves it time and time again. First Corinthians 2:9 says that no eye has seen and no ear has heard the wonderful things that God has prepared for you.

Today is your beginning. You have a divine destiny! You *have* a gift from God and you *are* a gift from God. You are special to God. And you should say as David did, *"I will praise thee; for I am fearfully and wonderfully made: marvellous are thy works; and that my soul knoweth right well"* (Ps. 139:14).

Each of us at one time or another has probably wanted to be something that we're not. Almost everyone has something they would like to change about themselves.

Well, God made us just the way He wanted us. And it's important not to criticize His workmanship! He made us perfect according to His specifications, so we can feel good about ourselves. We can say as David did, "Marvelous are Your works, O Lord." Or, in today's language, "Lord, You did a good job when You made me."

Don't criticize yourself—you are God's creation, His masterpiece! He has had a plan for your life from the very beginning. He has a special mission for you—a mission that only you can accomplish!

You may have started on that mission many years ago and have since taken a detour. Maybe you've taken several detours and have encountered many roadblocks along the way. You may have gotten so far off course that you think you will never find your way back.

Don't worry about finding your way back to God's plan for your life. You don't have to find your way to Him, because He found His way to you! It's as if God is saying, "I left the main road in order to find you. I am picking you up now and putting you back on your course in life."

God's Higher Way of Thinking and Better Way of Seeing

You may think you will never be a success in life, but God's thoughts about you are different. Your parents may have told you, "You're a slow learner, and you'll never amount to anything." But God's thoughts are different! You may have been told that you're not talented at anything. God's thoughts are different. You may have been told that you're not attractive and will never find a spouse. But God's thoughts are different.

God's plans for you are far greater than your plans for yourself. His ways are so much higher than your ways. You may think, *I will never be a leader. I'll always be a follower.* But God may have other plans for you. He needs leaders at various levels of life. His thoughts are different! You may think what you're doing now is all you will ever do in life. But God's thoughts are different! He has a higher way of thinking and a better way of seeing. So learn to think God's thoughts according to His Word to see yourself the way He sees you—as valuable and precious.

You may have acquired a lot of "baggage" along the path of life. Now you may think, *God, I have too much baggage to do anything worthwhile. I've made too many mistakes. I have so many scars from my life.* But the Lord is saying to you, "Your mistakes are forgiven, and your scars are healed." God does not hold your past against you. Jeremiah 29:11 says His plans are to give you hope and a *future*.

If God be for us, then who can be against us (Rom. 8:31)? With God on our side, there is no way that we can fail.

You may be called to teach or work in business. You may be called to be a parent and raise world-changers. You may be called to help your spouse reach his or her potential. When you're married, supporting your spouse is one of your primary responsibilities, but for some it can be a full-time calling. For those who have children, parenthood is definitely part of God's plan. But for some parents, raising a family may be a childhood dream, and they may have a special role to play in shaping future generations.

I use the ministry as my main example of a divine calling, because for me, full-time ministry is my calling in life. It is the destiny and plan that God had for me. So in those seasons when I wasn't in full-time ministry, I was tempted to wonder if I would ever fulfill my destiny and how the plans God spoke to me would ever come to pass.

Your calling may be different. Whatever your calling, the lessons are the same. We have a dream, or calling, in our heart and a plan from God for the future. But through life's seasons, we must wait on God's timing and direction in order to see His plan come to pass. We may get distracted or lose sight of the vision at times. That's why we must keep our hope in the Lord as we go through various seasons of life, trusting that He will indeed make our dreams come true.

Personal Prayer:

Father, I pray in faith, believing that Your will is being accomplished in my life. I thank You for meeting my needs and for placing within me all that I require to accomplish Your plan. I believe that You will never leave me or forsake me and that You are with me in every season of life. Instead of looking at the circum-

stances around me, I choose to look to You and to Your promises. You will bring Your Word to pass in my life, and I thank You for it now. In Jesus' Name, I pray. Amen.

CHAPTER 2

Successfully Handling the Seasons of Life

God has a plan for your life. Even at the very moment you were conceived, He had a plan and purpose for your future. Jeremiah 29:11 says, "'For I know the plans I have for you,' declares the Lord, 'plans to prosper you and not to harm you, plans to give you hope and a future'" (*NIV*).

Although God has a plan for you, He also gave you a free will, and you can choose whether or not you want to follow God's plan for your life. But if you want to be happy and satisfied, it's important that you walk according to the plan of God.

We all go through various seasons in life . . . in both our natural life and our spiritual life. In the natural, this may be your season to establish a career . . . or it may be the season to raise your children. I remember that season very well. It's a season of balancing all areas of your life. Many hours are spent attending school functions, going to ball games, and helping with school projects. During that season, there seems to be little time for your own pleasure!

But seasons change! For instance, I love my grandchildren . . . but I'm glad they're my grandchildren and not my children, because I've left that season of raising children! I'm now in what is called the "empty nest" season . . . and I love it!

I've told my husband that I've retired from cooking too, and while he loves my cooking, he is fine with that. When the kids were at home, I cooked every night. The evening meal was our family meal; dinnertime was when we fellowshipped and talked most as a family. But now that the kids are gone, I've retired from cooking!

I only come out of retirement for about two weeks a year during the Christmas holidays. That's when I cook my family's favorites: turkey and dressing, lasagna, chili, chicken-fried steak, salmon patties, and chicken and dumplings. I cook those dishes for about two weeks and invite the kids over. Then I tell them, "Okay, I've done my cooking for the year."

As I mentioned earlier, just as we go through natural seasons, we also experience spiritual seasons. Sometimes we're in a season of waiting; other times we're in a season of preparation for what God wants us to do. That can also include a time of gaining experience, and that's not always fun.

I'm reminded of a story about a successful business-man who was about to retire. A young executive was coming in to take his position.

The young executive asked, "Sir, could you tell me the secret of your success in business?"

The old man replied, "Just one thing, son, one thing—right decisions."

So the young man asked another question, "Well, sir, tell me, how do you learn to make right decisions?"

And the wise old man said, "Experience, son, experience."

This baffled the young man even more, so he asked, "But, sir, how do you gain experience?"

The old man replied, "Wrong decisions, son, wrong decisions."

That's a humorous story, but it's often a true fact: Many times we gain experience through our wrong decisions. The important thing is to learn from our mistakes and to make the *right* decision next time!

Spiritual Dry Seasons

There are also seasons of testing which will come and go throughout our life. The tests never completely end. And sometimes in the midst of testing, there are dry seasons.

Have you ever experienced a spiritual dry season—in other words, a time when you knew the Lord was with you, but you just couldn't feel His Presence? Those can be difficult times. I know we're supposed to walk by faith, but I like to have some feelings as well. During those dry seasons, I speak honestly with the Lord and tell Him, "God, I'm going to walk by faith, because I trust You and Your Word. But I want to have some feelings too. I have emotions, and I need to feel Your Presence."

Reaping Seasons

Although we sometimes go through dry seasons, praise the Lord, then comes the season of reaping! And I believe the season of reaping is about to occur for many—a reaping as never before.

As much as we all want to experience the season of reaping, we must pass through the first season before we can reach the next one. We must walk through life one step at a time, taking the first step before we take the next step.

And we can't go to the next season in our life until we are faithful in the first season.

Be Obedient to Take Your Place

When it comes to following God's plan for our life, some people only want to work where they can be seen. They don't want to follow God's plan if it means being behind the scenes. Some people will do what God wants them to do if it means they can give orders and be in charge of others. Then there are other people who just want to do what they want to do, when they want to do it! If God's plan is inconvenient for them, then forget it!

But if we're going to prepare for the Second Coming of Christ, we must be willing to do whatever it takes to reach the lost. There is a lost and dying world out there that needs a Savior, and in order to reach them, each one of us must be willing to take our individual place in the Kingdom of God. We must be willing to fulfill God's plan for our life. Walking out God's plan will not only make us happy and satisfied in our own life, but we will then make a difference in the lives of others and help make ready Christ's return!

One behind-the-scenes job that is vitally important is *prayer*. Prayer is one of the most important things any person can do. Many times pray-ers don't get a lot of recognition from man. But when the rewards are passed out in Heaven, everyone will know what these pray-ers accomplished for the Lord.

We may be surprised at the many rewards lavished on the precious people who were consumed with praying for the needs of the Church and of others. The rewards may be stacked high simply because they were faithful to pray.

During the time in my life when my place in ministry seemed so far away, all I could do was pray. Of course, one thing I prayed about concerned my call in life. I prayed, "Lord, walk me through the steps of what You would have me to do in ministry."

Then I told the Lord, "I don't mind praying. I love to pray. But I also love to speak into people's lives and to make a difference that way. I love to give to people. I love to see people helped. I don't have to have a pulpit ministry. I love one-on-one ministry. You could use me that way."

But the next season of my life in ministry wasn't going to be pulpit ministry or one-on-one ministry. It was going to be something that I never thought of as ministry and something I didn't think I could ever do—interior decorating and design!

'I Don't Want to Decorate!'

It was 1976, and we had just moved Kenneth Hagin Ministries to the RHEMA campus, where it is still located today. In 1976, there was only one building and a warehouse, so we had to start adding buildings in order to house every department of the ministry and RHEMA Bible Training Center classes.

My husband was active in the ministry then, while I was at home raising Craig and Denise. Then Ken said to me, "It's time to choose paint, carpet, furniture, and so forth, and we don't have anyone to do that. You're going to have to do it."

Now I had been praying, "Lord, use me. Use me!" When I prayed, "Lord, I'll do what You want me to do; I'll go where You want me to go; I'll say what You want me to say," interior decorating wasn't what I had in mind! I was expecting some kind of pastoral ministry, and the Lord said, "Go pick out wallpaper and carpet."

I was honest with the Lord and told Him, "God, I really don't mind doing this, except it's something I've never desired to do. Besides that, I don't even feel as though I'm qualified to do this kind of work. I don't know how to choose carpet. I don't know how to choose wallpaper. But if that's what You want, that's what I'll do! I'll do whatever You want me to do."

So I began choosing carpet, paint, and wallpaper, and doing one decorating job after another. Then one day I asked the Lord, "Why are You using me in this area? I feel so inadequate! I feel so unqualified! Why didn't You ask me to organize something? I'm a good organizer. You know I love those to-do lists. You know I can set up any office. Why don't You let me work in the office? I don't want to decorate. I want to work in the office!"

I'll never forget His answer the longest day I live. He said, "That's the problem, Lynette. You want to do what you feel comfortable with. I need you to listen to My voice. I have put you outside of your comfort zone so that you can learn to hear My voice. I will teach you supernaturally how to decorate. You must learn to listen to My voice, because the job that I have for you to do is greater than your ability."

I used to have nightmares when I first started decorating the buildings. In my dreams, thousands and thousands of people would walk into the building, look around, and say, "Yuck! Who decorated this?"

But, praise God, His ways are higher than our ways! He helped me complete the task. And I remember the time some people who were professional decorators visited the campus and saw the lobby of Student Development Center I. When they said the building was beautifully decorated, I knew they were bragging on my God!

God Knows What He's Doing

In 1976, decorating was a job beyond my natural ability. God knew that when He asked me to do it. But if I hadn't followed His directions and learned to hear His voice concerning decorating, no one would have really been the worse for it. I mean, the walls and carpet may have been ugly, but no one would have been hurt by my work.

However, if I hadn't followed God's directions and learned to hear His voice concerning decorating, *I* would have been affected. Because if I hadn't learned then and in that situation to hear God's voice and to follow His leading, I would have never stepped into the next season He had planned for me.

You see, God knew that the ministry He had ultimately called me to do was also beyond my ability. He knew that He would have to supernaturally teach me to do what I'm doing today. And He knew that in order for me to get the job done, I had to learn to stop relying on my own strength and start relying on His.

My first steps were small. As I was faithful to walk through the season of motherhood, God led me to pray. As I was faithful to walk through the season of prayer, God led me to the season of decorating the ministry buildings. As I was faithful in what seemed like little things to me, God led me along His path for my life and to all that I had desired in my heart.

You may have already realized that the job God has called you to do is greater than your ability. Or you may still be relying on your own strength. But to fulfill your divine destiny, you must rely on God's strength. And it's not difficult to do. Praise God, He has placed His ability on the inside of you, and if you will tap into it, you will have the grace to do whatever it is He has called you to do!

Seasons of Testing

Most of us acknowledge the fact that God's abilities are greater than our abilities. When the season of testing comes, we must rely on God's abilities, not on our own. Our own strength won't see us through, but God's strength will.

No one likes the season of testing. It's a season we experience at different times throughout our life, because our adversary, the devil, continues to go around seeking whom he may devour (1 Peter 5:8). Just remember, he can't devour you if you won't allow him to!

Many times during seasons of testing, I've been prompted to read James chapter 1. This passage always serves to encourage me during hard times.

JAMES 1:2–4 (*NIV*)

2   Consider it pure joy, my brothers, whenever you face trials of many kinds,

3   because you know that the testing of your faith develops perseverance.

4   Perseverance must finish its work so that you may be mature and complete, not lacking anything.

Tests and trials are not fun. In and of themselves, trials are not joyful at all! It's only because you know the end result that you can consider trials to be joy. So if you're going through a trial, consider it joy! Why? Because you know that the testing of your faith develops perseverance.

Sometimes when a test came, I've wanted to say, "God, this is not worth it. It's too hard, and I just want to give up!" But each time those natural thoughts came to me, the Greater One on the inside of me said, "But My thoughts are higher than your thoughts. My ways are higher than your ways."

Thoughts of doubt, despair, and depression will come to us all. But it's what we do with those thoughts that matter. When those thoughts come to you, when you are feeling depressed about whatever situation you're going through, remember that God cares about you. He knows what you're going through, and He is there to help you through the trial you're facing.

'I Can Do All Things'

One of my favorite scriptures—one that has gotten me through many battles in life—is Philippians 4:13, which says, *"I can do all things through Christ which strengtheneth me."* Notice this verse doesn't say, "I can do *some* things." It says, "I can do *all* things"! In other words, whatever God has planned for me to do in life, He has also given me the strength to do it. With Him, I can do all the things He has called me to do. I just need to look to Him and believe His Word is true!

There have been times when I confessed Philippians 4:13 just because I knew God's Word was true. I didn't feel as though I could do all things, and my voice was pretty weak while making my confession. But the more I said it, the stronger my confession became. The more I quoted

God's Word, the stronger *I* became. Eventually, I gained the confidence I needed to get through that crisis of life.

If You Need Wisdom, Ask for It!

There are many times in life when we need wisdom—a supernatural wisdom that is beyond our own thoughts or ideas. I know I need that kind of wisdom on a daily basis. So I appropriate James 1:5, which says, "If any of you lacks wisdom, he should ask God, who gives generously to all without finding fault, and it will be given to him" (*NIV*).

The Bible says that when we need wisdom, we should ask God for it. God will give *generously* to us, without finding fault with us or reprimanding us for lacking wisdom. However, there is one condition. When we ask God for His wisdom, we must accept the wisdom He gives and not doubt it.

JAMES 1:6–8 (*NIV*)

6   But when he asks, he must believe and not doubt, because he who doubts is like a wave of the sea, blown and tossed by the wind.

7   That man should not think he will receive anything from the Lord;

8   he is a double-minded man, unstable in all he does.

Has God ever given you wisdom, or the answer to something you asked Him about, and you questioned Him about what He told you? Sometimes I've said, "But, God, that couldn't possibly be what I'm supposed to do! That just couldn't be the answer to my problems!" I was being double-minded. I wanted God's wisdom, but when He gave it to me, I didn't want to receive it. I still wanted to follow my own ideas. When God gives you wisdom, take it! When He gives you the answer, receive it!

The Crisis That Challenged My Faith

Crises will come to each of us; it's what we do in those crises that matters. One of the greatest crises that we've experienced in our life occurred in January 1983, when our son, Craig, was in the eighth grade.

Because he had been having headaches, we had taken Craig to the doctor. They thought it might be his sinuses, so they took X-rays and ran various tests. Everything tested normal, and the doctors could not find anything wrong.

Yet on the inside of me, I knew something was happening. Craig was not himself; he was normally a happy child. I knew something was wrong.

As long as I live, I'll never forget the night my suspicions were confirmed. We were awakened in the middle of the night by an awful scream. My husband stumbled up the stairs to Craig's room and found him lying on the floor, holding his head and screaming, "My head, my head, my head!"

Then Craig vomited and felt some relief from the agonizing pain. We got him back into bed and he slept the rest of the night. But then we knew for sure that something was desperately wrong.

The next day, we took Craig to the doctor, who ran additional tests to determine the problem. Later, five doctors were in the room with us when we were told, "Your son has a brain tumor the size of a lemon. It's located right against his brain stem. One impact could end his life."

The scariest thing was the fact that Craig had been playing contact football during this time. He was scheduled to start in the next game, so he would have been involved in a lot of physical contact. When we learned of Craig's life-threatening condition and that any impact could kill him, football no longer mattered. In fact, nothing mattered.

At that moment, the importance of houses, cars, clothes, jewelry, and everything else in life faded away. Nothing mattered but the life of my son. I thought, *Lord, could I please take my son's place? I don't want it to be my precious baby who goes through this.*

My husband and I prayed. My family prayed. But there was no change. Then my father-in-law said something to me that buoyed my spirit. He said, "You know, an army never goes out to battle without a second line of defense."

That's when my husband and I shifted our faith. Our first line of defense had been supernatural divine healing. But we were going to be as wise as a natural army and form a second line of defense. We still kept our faith in God, but we also determined to do whatever we could in the natural to win the battle!

We put our faith out that God would direct the doctors' hands as they removed the tumor. We believed the surgery would go well and that there wouldn't be any complications or side effects. We also believed that the brain tumor would be benign, not malignant.

God Hears and Answers Prayer

Craig stayed in the hospital as the surgeons prepared for surgery. I knew we would also stay at the hospital the entire time Craig was there, so I went back home to pack clothes for him as well as for my husband and me.

In my closet, I prayed, "God, I need to feel You right now. I know we walk by faith, and I am in faith. But I need to hear Your voice. I need to feel You. I need You to speak to me. I need the comfort of the Holy Spirit to let me know everything is going to be okay."

Of course, I knew in my heart that everything was going to be okay, but I needed to feel God's Presence at that moment because of the enormity of the situation. And God is so precious to grant our desires.

As I was praying, something fell from a shelf in my closet. It was very small, but I was curious to know what it was, so I bent down to see what had fallen. My carpet was pretty thick, so it was amazing that I found it—a tiny lapel pin.

'You Can Make It'

A few months earlier, my husband and I had ministered in North Carolina. This little lapel pin was a gift we had received while on that trip. For some reason, it was on that shelf in my closet and had fallen at just the right time. When I turned the pin over to see what it was, I saw that it said, "You can make it."

It was like an audible voice from God to me! *You can make it.* I thanked the Lord for answering my prayer.

Hey, God, Why Is It Taking So Long?

I went to the hospital room where Craig was waiting for surgery and told him about the pin. I said, "Son, the Lord has just dropped a pin from Heaven! He says, 'You can make it.' We're going to pin this on you. And if fear tries to grip you while you're in the operating room, you just remember that pin. You remember that you are going to make it!"

When the doctors came out to us after 12 hours of surgery, I didn't need to hear what they had to say. My confidence was in what God had said. I knew that Craig was going to make it!

The doctors told us it was a textbook surgery. I asked them what that meant, and they said, "No instrument was dropped. Nothing went wrong." In fact, the two nurses who assisted the anesthesiologists were followers of our ministry. One of them had a chronic back condition which was healed during the surgery by the power of God which was so strong in the room.

God hears and answers prayer! We believed for the surgery to go well with no complications or side effects, and our faith was rewarded. We believed that God would guide the surgeons' hands, and He did. I believed for a word from Heaven to comfort me in my time of need, and God heard my cry and answered me. *You can make it!*

Our son, Craig, is now a grown man who has graduated from college and from RHEMA Bible Training Center. He has three children of his own and works with us in the ministry. Praise God! What the enemy meant for evil, God turned around for our good.

Romans 8:28 says, "And we know that in all things God works for the good of those who love him, who have been called according to his purpose" (*NIV*). I don't know what trial may have come your way, but whatever it is, God will deliver you. And that which the enemy meant for evil, God will turn around for your good.

I want to tell you, "You can make it!" If you have been tormented by fear of any kind, the Lord wants to set you free so that fear can no longer abide or reside in your life. That which you have been tormented by will be gone, and you shall be as a brand-new person. The Lord God will keep you in perfect peace as you trust in Him and keep your mind steadfastly on Him (Isa. 26:3).

CHAPTER 3

Commit, Prepare, Wait, Prove

In following the plan of God for your life, there are many seasons that you will go through. Just as there are natural seasons throughout the calendar year, there are seasons throughout the years of life.

Now, I am an organizer by nature; I like everything in my life to be in a particular order. And I really would prefer that God give me a detailed 10-year plan for my life! I would even settle for a 5-year plan! Many can probably relate. But I found that God usually does not give us advance plans. He wants us to walk by faith and not by sight (2 Cor. 5:7). So we have to follow His plan one step at a time.

Just naturally speaking, there are some seasons that I like better than others. And there are some seasons I don't like much at all. For example, I don't like winter. Spring is okay, but it rains a lot during that season, and I don't like rainy weather because it's humid, and my hair falls! So spring is just *okay* with me. I don't mind the heat, so summer is okay too. But my favorite season is autumn. It doesn't rain too much in the fall; it's not humid; it's not cold; and it's not hot. To me the fall season is just right, so I always look forward to that time of year.

In our natural lives, there are different seasons: childhood, youth, adulthood, midlife, retirement age, and so forth. Each person may have his or her own opinion as to which "season" of life is best. As I mentioned in Chapter 2, we also have *spiritual* seasons in life. In this chapter, I want to talk more in-depth about those seasons and will deal specifically with four seasons: (1) the season of *commitment*; (2) the season of *preparation*; (3) the season of *waiting*; and (4) the season of *proving*.

The Season of *Commitment*

The first season I want to talk about is the season of *commitment*. To walk out the plan of God for our life, we must walk through the season of commitment.

Even Jesus had to walk through this season to fulfill the plan of God for His life. John 6:38 says, *"For I came down from heaven, not to do my mine own will but the will of him that sent me."* Jesus didn't come to this earth to do His own thing and follow His own plan. He came to do the will of His Father.

Jesus didn't necessarily want to be the Supreme Sacrifice and to die a horrific death on the Cross. In fact, in Matthew 26:39, Jesus prayed, *"O my Father, if it be possible, let this cup pass from me: nevertheless not as I will, but as thou wilt."* Regardless of what Jesus Himself wanted to do, the primary thing He wanted to do was to do the will of the Father. He said, "Not My will, but *Thy* will be done."

It was a sacrifice for the Lord Jesus Christ to make the *commitment* to do the will of the Father. And if it was difficult for *Jesus* to commit to the will of the Father, we will most definitely find it difficult at times, won't we?

It's sometimes difficult to commit to doing things God's way, because we want it our way. We want to have our will be done, not God's will.

When I was a child, altars were common in most churches. I remember going down to the altar in my church nearly every service. That altar always reminded me of surrendering to the will of God. And I remember singing the song "I Surrender All" many, many times (nearly every service).

We were taught to surrender and consecrate our will to God's will. We were encouraged to not only bring our requests to the altar (every service, we went down to the altar to pray), but to commit our lives to God—to commit to doing His will and to following His plan.

The altar was a sacred place. It was a place of commitment. Sometimes it seems that along with removing the physical altars from churches, we have removed the commitment from our lives that those altars symbolized.

It seems we just want to hear the Word, believe the Word, confess the Word, and receive from the Word. If we're not careful, we will start following man's formula for this. Truth becomes head knowledge instead of heart knowledge. That's why some people don't receive what they say they're believing for—because they're trying to operate a formula that they don't really believe. They are just mimicking someone with the words of their mouth instead of believing God for themselves and speaking from their heart.

In this day and age, many people ignore the ideas of commitment and consecration. I think the word "commitment" has almost disappeared from our vocabulary. We don't want to commit to anything. People don't even R.S.V.P. for parties anymore! They think, *When that day comes, if I feel like going, I'll go. But I might not feel like going, so I don't want to commit to going right now.* And so they don't answer an invitation that asks for a response. People don't want to commit!

But commitment is very, very important. It's important in the affairs of life, and it's important in your walk with God.

Although Abraham was blessed of God, he never forgot his commitment to God. He was even willing to sacrifice his son if that's what God asked him to do (*see* Genesis 22). Abraham never questioned God; he simply obeyed Him.

In God's design, three things must take place in a certain order if we are to successfully fulfill God's divine plan for our lives. First, we must be willing to commit to the plan of God. Second, God will reveal the plan. And then, third, we must walk out the plan. But so many times, we want to put God's design in reverse order. We want to know what the plan is before we will commit to it.

Afraid of Being a Missionary

As a little girl, I was so afraid that God was going to call me to be a missionary. I did not want to be a missionary, because I had heard the testimonies of every missionary who came to our church. They usually had no electricity, no running water, no nothing! I'm a city girl. I need electricity, and I need water. I need shopping malls and restaurants!

Hey, God, Why Is It Taking So Long?

I was so afraid that if I committed my all to the Lord, He would ask me to be a missionary. As we would sing, "I surrender all . . . ," I would silently pray, "But, God, *please* don't ask me to be a missionary. *Please* don't ask me to be a missionary."

Every time a missionary came to the church, I just cried and cried and cried, thinking God was going to ask me to be a missionary. Don't misunderstand me. I think missionaries are important—the ministry they provide is invaluable. It didn't make sense to me why I reacted the way I did, because I just loved to hear their stories of touching people's lives. But I myself did not want to be a missionary. I think I walked in fear that God would ask me to be one.

Then about 15 years ago, a missionary came to RHEMA Bible Church in Broken Arrow, Oklahoma, where my husband is the pastor, and there I was boo-hooing again, thinking, *God, please don't call us to be missionaries.*

I'll never forget that day because at the end of the service, my husband said something that set my heart free. He said, "You can have a *heart* for missions without having a *call* for missions." Suddenly, it all made sense! I thought, *Yes, Lord! You just gave me my answer through my husband. That's why the stories touch my heart, yet I don't want to go on the mission field. I have a heart for missions, but I don't have a call for missions.* God uses various ways to speak His answers to your questions.

Grace to Do It

All God wants from us is for us to be a willing vessel—wholly committed to Him. And whatever He asks us to do, He will give us the grace to do it!

So many people have asked me, "How do you do what you do? I couldn't do it." No, they probably couldn't do exactly what I do, because God didn't call them to do it. He has called *me* to do it. And because He has called me, He has given me the grace! Believe me, I couldn't do what I do in my own strength. My faith is in the power of God, and I can do all things through Him who strengthens me (1 Cor. 2:5; Phil. 4:13). I walk in grace and peace only because I am following the plan of God for my life.

When you follow the plan of God for *your* life, you will walk in grace and peace. *And* you will walk in the determination that no matter what it takes, you are committed to fulfilling what God has for you.

It takes willingness and commitment to follow God's plan for our life. It would be terrible for us to stand in front of the Judgment Seat of Christ and hear Him say, "Half well-done, thou half-good and half-faithful servant."

Hey, God, Why Is It Taking So Long?

It's not true commitment if it's only *halfway*. We must *fully* commit to following God's will for our lives.

I will admit that it takes effort to walk out that commitment on a daily basis. There are constant opportunities to go back on our commitment. For instance, when someone wrongs us, we want to hold a grudge. We want to give that offender a piece of our mind! And if we allow ourselves to get in the flesh, that's exactly what we will do!

But when we follow the plan of God, we are committed to doing what He has asked us to do. So instead of giving people a piece of our mind (which we will have many opportunities to do), we must choose to obey the Word which says, *"Bless them that curse you, and pray for them which despitefully use you"* (Luke 6:28).

It may seem like a trivial matter, but in order to be committed to God's plan for our life, we must be willing to obey His Word in *every* area. When we obey God's Word concerning loving our neighbor and forgiving our enemies, we will be more likely to obey God's voice when He tells us His plan for our life.

When you're offered a job that would appear to fulfill your dreams, yet God tells you it's not the job to take, you will find out whether or not you're committed to God.

44

When God asks you to do something that you don't really want to do, you'll find out if you're committed or not!

The Moment of Truth—Another Test of Commitment

I remember going to the altar as a young girl and praying, "Lord, I'll go where You want me to go. I'll do what You want me to do. I'll say what You want me to say." Praying that prayer, I felt so blessed and close to God, because I thought, *I have just committed my all to the Lord.* I felt so good!

And for about the first 27 years of my life, I prayed that joyfully, "Lord, I'm committed to You. I'll go where You want me to go," until one day God asked me to go somewhere I didn't want to go and to do something I didn't want to do. That's when I found out how committed I really was.

At that moment I had a decision to make. I could follow my plans and do what I wanted to do—what *I* had planned for my life. Or I could follow the will of God for my life. Quite frankly, it was not an easy decision to make.

At that time, my husband and I worked as associate pastors for my father, Rev. V.E. Tipton. And I loved being a pastor's wife. I was comfortable in that role because my dad had been a pastor all my life. I always thought that was what God would want me to do.

Hey, God, Why Is It Taking So Long?

When I was in college, I was a member of a traveling singing group. On the road we stayed in guest homes and always had a roommate. I remember once telling my roommate, "I will never marry an evangelist." I knew even then that I was going to marry a minister; I always knew that. But I said, "I will never marry an evangelist, because I cannot stand to travel." I was a homebody, and I loved being at home!

So it was a dark day in my life when the Lord told my husband, "It's time to go to the next level of your ministry." First, it meant leaving Texas, which had been my home my entire life, to move to Oklahoma. I would miss the big cities, great shopping, and so many restaurants! And Texas and Oklahoma are football rivals! I thought, *Lord! Surely not!* On top of all that, we were to leave pastoral ministry and begin traveling with my father-in-law, Rev. Kenneth E. Hagin.

All my nightmares were coming true! Leaving Texas! Moving to Oklahoma! Traveling! *And* we were going to be living (me, my husband, and our 3-year-old son) in a 31-foot motor home for months at a time!

That was the day I discovered how committed I really was. But I had been taught about the dangers of living outside of God's will. So at that time, probably more out of fear than anything else, I chose to follow God. I knew I didn't want to be out of God's will for my life.

But I remember saying to the Lord, "Lord, You've revealed this to my husband, and he says this is what we're supposed to do. But, God, I need to know that for myself. I need to know that this is Your plan for our life."

I know the Bible tells wives to submit to their husbands (Eph. 5:22; Col. 3:18). And I do what the Bible says. I believe that wives *should* go where their husbands say go. But I told the Lord, "I believe that if You've told *him*, You can also tell *me*."

Knowing for Myself

Sometimes the problem is that women don't want to listen and hear what God has to say, because they want to follow their own plans. Men also need to be sure they've heard from God before uprooting a family from familiar surroundings. But I was a willing vessel, wholly committed to following God, so I said, "God, if this is what we're supposed to do, tell me as well, because I have *to know that I know that I know.*"

One of the reasons I had *to know that I know* is because I knew what a powerful influence wives have on their husbands. It's been said, "If Momma ain't happy, ain't nobody happy!" Women can make life miserable for their whole family.

Hey, God, Why Is It Taking So Long?

In my particular instance, because I'd been raised in the ministry, I knew the time would come in my husband's life when the enemy would try to discourage him, saying, "You didn't really hear from God. You're not doing what God called you to do. You just made a mistake and heard incorrectly."

I knew that time would come because the enemy will always try to steer us off course—off the plan of God for our life. And I knew that if I personally did not know for myself that God had told my husband to make this change, when the enemy came to discourage Ken, I would have sided on the wrong side! I would have said to him, "I told you so. I knew we were not supposed to do this. Let's go back to Texas."

Sometimes we just need to be honest with ourselves. I knew myself well enough to know that I would do that. I'm a strong-willed woman, and that's okay as long as I use that strong will the right way. In other words, I need to use my will against the enemy, not against my husband! So I said, "God, if You showed him, I ask You to please show me too."

To make a long story short, through prayer and reading the Word, God showed me exactly what I was to do. I was to follow my husband because, yes, he had correctly heard God's plan for our life. And so we went—and I was happy about it. There were times when I was thankful that

I was committed. Otherwise, I may have regretted the decision. But I learned to say, "Lord, it's okay if I live in Oklahoma. Just please bring some shopping malls to this city!" And He did!

Seriously, it was important that I heard from God for myself and was fully committed to obeying Him, because it wasn't but a few months later that my husband became discouraged. At that time I was able to say, "No, honey, you didn't miss it. We're doing what God has called us to do, and we're going to keep on doing it."

Make Your Commitment Right Now

Are you willing to commit to God's call on your life? If you're willing to do what it takes to answer the call, make this confession: "I willingly commit to following God's plan for my life. Lord, I commit myself to You right now—not just 99 percent, but 100 percent. I am forever a willing vessel, ready to do whatever You have called and created me to do."

Somewhere you need to write down the commitment you just made. Write it down—in a journal, in a diary, in your Bible—somewhere you can easily find it and read it. Then when doubts come to your mind about whether or not you should follow God's plan or your own plan, or when the enemy tries to distract you from your divine purpose, you can remind yourself of the commitment you have made.

Determine right now that nothing will keep you from God's high calling. Borrowing a sports analogy, the time for practice is over. This is game time! It's going to take a commitment of commitments to run the race God has for you. This world, especially our current culture, is full of distractions. It's going to take extreme focus to stay in the race. Just as a racehorse wears blinders to successfully compete, we, too, must wear "blinders." We must not look to the left or to the right, but we must keep our eyes on the prize.

The Season of *Preparation*

The first season we must weather is the season of *commitment*. We must get to the place in our spiritual walk where, no matter what, we are committed to doing the will of God. The second season is the season of *preparation*.

After committing to the will of God, a season of preparation follows. James 4:8 says, *"Draw nigh to God, and he will draw nigh to you. . . ."* The Amplified Bible says, "Come close to God and He will come close to you."

If we're going to *follow* the plan of God for our life, we must develop a relationship with our Heavenly Father so He can tell us what the plan *is*. We develop that relationship through prayer and through reading and meditating on His Word. Joshua 1:8 says, "Do not let this Book of the Law depart from your mouth; meditate on it day and night, so that you may be careful to do everything written in it. Then you will be prosperous and successful" (*NIV*).

If you're going to do the will of God and follow His plan for your life, you're going to have to walk closely enough to Him to hear His commands, and the only way to do that is to draw near to Him. The nearer you are to Him, the clearer His voice becomes.

The Lord wants to be our Best Friend. He will never tell any of our secrets, and He is kind and ever-patient with us. He loves us even when we are "unlovely." That's a friend indeed!

We're all human, and many times we neglect reading the Word. We neglect praying until a crisis occurs. Then we fall on our knees and get the Bible out and start reading God's promises. We say, "Oh God, help me, help me, help me" when, really, we should have been communing with Him and reading His Word all along. Had we been doing that, we might not have had the crisis to begin with!

Unfortunately, we humans want to wait until we fall into a crisis. But we must learn to prepare, to walk through the season of preparation *now*, so that we're ready when the crises of life come to us or when the Lord calls on us to do something big for Him.

When any sports team gets far behind an opponent during a game, they will usually become tentative and play in a defensive manner for the rest of the game. Instead of playing to win, the losing team becomes tentative and must play catch-up! It's harder to catch up than it is to maintain a lead. It's much better to be on the offensive in sports and in life.

It also makes good natural sense to have the house built before the rain comes! It's been said that you can't lay a foundation in the middle of a flood. And that's true in more ways than one. It's true in a natural sense, and it's true in a spiritual sense, including our prayer life.

If it takes a crisis for us to pray, then we're "playing catch-up" all the time. In other words, we're praying from a reactive or defensive mode instead of being on the offensive in our prayer life and in our Christian walk.

Talking to God and Hearing His Voice

Matthew 6:33 says, *"But seek ye first the kingdom of God, and his righteousness; and all these things shall be added unto you."* All my life I was taught to seek the Kingdom of God first. What does "seek first the Kingdom of God" mean? One thing it means is that we put our relationship with God above everything else in life. Building a strong and intimate relationship with God takes time and effort.

The season of preparation takes time. It takes time to learn how to communicate with our Heavenly Father just as it takes time to learn to communicate in natural relationships. Communication skills do not come easy. Clear communication is often one of the most difficult things in life to achieve. Many times, what people hear us say is not what we mean at all! Sometimes it seems that no matter what wives say, their husbands usually hear something else. (Husbands say their wives do the same thing!)

My husband and I have had to learn how to properly communicate with one another when doing something as simple as giving driving directions. We give directions in totally different ways. The way I tend to give directions confuses him, and the way he gives directions confuses me. Men and women think so differently!

My husband and I have been married more than 38 years. We love each other, and we even like to be around each other. We like to share life with each other. But we still had to learn to communicate with each other in a way that the other person would understand. Just because we said "I do" at the wedding altar didn't mean that our communication was instantly perfect.

Hey, God, Why Is It Taking So Long?

In fact, the way my husband and I first communicated with each other was far from perfect. It has taken us a lot of time to develop our communication skills. But the time and effort we put into developing a communication system have been worth it. Now after so many years of being together, we have started to think alike in a lot of ways, and that makes communicating a little easier.

It's the same way with our Heavenly Father. Just because we got saved didn't mean that our communication with God was instantly perfect. We still need to learn how to commune with Him. And with time and effort, we can develop intimate communication with God. The goal is to spend so much time with God that we eventually begin to think like Him, talk like Him, and act like Him!

Many times, mothers have a special ability to understand their children. When a child is young and no one else can understand what he's saying, his mom can. Mothers have a gift for understanding their child's gibberish, partly because moms usually spend more time with that child than any other person does. Moms have learned to understand the language.

The same thing happens with the Heavenly Father. The more time we spend with Him, the better we will be able to understand what He's saying to us. When we are first developing in our communication with the Heavenly

Father, we're not quite tuned into what He's saying. Maybe His voice sounds muffled or unclear to us, much like a child's gibberish might sound to non-discerning adults. But unlike a child, it isn't God Who speaks unclearly. It's we who aren't listening properly. But as we commune with God more, we will better understand His voice.

I don't mean that God will necessarily speak out loud to us. He often speaks to us through the still, small voice inside—in our spirit. At other times, He will speak to us through Scripture while we're reading the Bible, or He'll bring something to our remembrance in a time of need. Of course, anything God tells us will always line up with His written Word. If what we're "hearing" doesn't line up with God's Word, it isn't God who's speaking to us.

We don't have to be down on our knees for God to talk to us. He talks to me many times when I'm in the shower, putting on my makeup, or driving in my car, because I use those times to meditate on Him and His Word. I use those alone moments to commune with Him.

God Can Speak to Us Through Other People

Sometimes God will speak to us through other people. A great example of this was when the dean of RHEMA Bible Training Center resigned several years ago, and I was wondering whom to hire in his place. His resignation was a dark day in my life, because he had been with our ministry for 20 years. I thought he would never leave; then, suddenly, he was leaving! We were happy for where God was taking him in ministry, but I remember thinking, *Oh my goodness! Who's going to take his place, Lord?*

I started praying only when I heard he was leaving, because I had to know the will of God about the situation. But, you see, had I been more sensitive to God's voice, I could have been prepared ahead of time. I wouldn't have been caught off guard.

While I was praying, no one's name seemed to come up in my spirit concerning a replacement. Then one day, not long after I began praying about it, I was having a meeting with one of our employees. He said to me, "I was talking to So-and-so the other day, and he told me that he was feeling a tug to come back to RHEMA."

At that particular time, no one knew the dean was leaving. I had kept it a secret because I was in a dilemma. I knew if I made it public, I would receive about 500 applications for the job and I didn't want to have to go through 500 applications! I wanted the will of God.

Now this name the employee had given me had crossed my mind, but I dismissed it thinking, *No, they love being missionaries. They were here once and left to be missionaries, and they love being on the mission field.* I remembered trying to talk them out of leaving before they ever went to the mission field! So I figured it was a lost cause to try to talk them into coming back.

But even though I had dismissed the thought, God brought someone along my path with the message. To make a long story short, when I mentioned the position to the missionary and his family, they gladly accepted and have done a fine job at RBTC!

If you sincerely want to hear God's voice and learn to be sensitive to Him, He will find a way to speak to you. Some of the ways God speaks to us are through the inward witness, through the Word, through other people, and, sometimes, through circumstances. The bottom line is, we need to be sensitive to hear His voice so that no matter how He chooses to speak to us, we are always listening and ready to obey. (I will talk more about following the leading of the Spirit in Chapter 4.)

The season of preparation is the perfect time to develop a strong relationship with the Heavenly Father, so when the inevitable storms of life do come, our foundation in God has already been made secure.

The Season of *Waiting*

The first season I covered in this chapter is *commitment*; the second season is *preparation*, and the third season is the season of *waiting*. Psalm 46:10 says, *"Be still, and know that I am God. . . ."*

We don't like to hear about the season of waiting because waiting is not something we like to do. People today want instant everything: instant food, instant service, instant gratification. We don't want to wait for anything; we want everything in a hurry. But God never gets in a hurry.

When cooking a pot of beans, in order for them to taste best, I always add seasonings to the pot and then just let the beans keep cooking, sometimes for hours. Over time, the seasonings soak into the beans, adding a delicious flavor. Cooking the beans for a long time makes them taste much better than cooking them quickly.

Whenever we think God is not moving quickly enough, we should tell ourselves that He is seasoning us! Everything will turn out great if we will just learn how to wait. Isaiah 40:31 says, *"But they that wait upon the Lord shall renew their strength; they shall mount up with wings as eagles; they shall run, and not be weary; and they shall walk, and not faint."*

Waiting for God's Timing

If you are weary and don't have a lot of strength, maybe you aren't waiting on the Lord as much as you should. I will admit, it is hard to learn how to wait on the Lord. We want to hurry things along, but if we do, we can get out of His season or timing. It's so important for us to develop patience and wait for God's plan in His timing.

It was more than 30 years ago that I really started praying and asking God for His plan for my life. He told me then that one of my ministries would be to minister to the needs of women. I waited and waited to see that plan come to pass.

Now, I knew at age 29 that I still needed some seasoning! So I thought, *When I'm 40, this will come to pass.* But when I turned 40, God still said the timing wasn't right. I still needed to wait upon the Lord. So I thought, *Surely when I'm 50!* I waited another 10 years. At 50, I thought, *Now is the time!* But God said, "No." It wasn't until I was 56 that God said, "Now is the time." He defined the plan more clearly at this time when He said, "I will gather an army of women around you, and it will be a mighty force in the last days."

From the time God revealed to me His plan to the time God's plan came to pass took 27 years. In 2001, I hosted the first annual *Kindle the Flame* Women's Conference. Gathered with me that year, and each year since, were hundreds of women from around the world, a company or army of women, a mighty force for God!

If I had walked in the wrong season, following my own timing, the plan of God would not have been carried out. In other words, if I had run with the plan at 29, at 40, or at 50, I would have missed God's timing, and the plan would have failed. If we want to walk in the perfect will of God, it's just as important to know God's *timing* as it is to know God's *plan*.

Don't Jump Out of the Boat!

It's so important for us to learn to wait on God and His timing. Sometimes He is keeping us still for just the right season. It's hard to be still; we all get fidgety. We often jump out of the boat before God can take us safely to the other side!

What if the disciples in Mark chapter 4 had gotten fidgety and jumped ship? They were on a boat crossing to the other side when a storm arose midway through their journey. Of course, Jesus was sleeping through the storm. What if the disciples had grown impatient and jumped out of the boat? Then Jesus couldn't have said, "Peace, be still" (Mark 4:39).

Jesus might be saying to you right now, "Peace, be still." And you may be trying to jump out of the boat. If you jump out of the boat, you may drown! It's so important to be patient and to wait for God—to go through the season of waiting and follow God's timing.

The Seasons of *Proving*

After *commitment*, *preparation*, and *waiting*, there always comes the season of *proving*. Oh, the waiting is bad enough! But *tests*? No! We don't want to be tested, do we?

JAMES 1:2–4 (*Amplified*)

2 Consider it wholly joyful, my brethren, whenever you are enveloped in or encounter trials of any sort or fall into various temptations.

3 Be assured and understand that the trial and proving of your faith bring out endurance and steadfastness and patience.

4 But let endurance and steadfastness and patience have full play and do a thorough work, so that you may be [people] perfectly and fully developed [with no defects], lacking in nothing.

Hey, God, Why Is It Taking So Long?

God did not promise that life would be a bed of roses. There will be tests along the road of life. There will be proving seasons. But during those times of testing, we can build our faith and our endurance.

There can't be a victory without a battle. In life there will be tests and trials, but you don't have to worry. In John 16:33, Jesus said, "I have told you these things, so that in me you may have peace. In this world you will have trouble. But take heart! I have overcome the world" (*NIV*). And James 1:3 says, "Be assured and understand that the trial and proving of your faith bring out endurance and steadfastness and patience" (*Amplified*).

✓ The past couple of years or so have been a real testing time for many. I hear it from people all over the country— the enemy has attacked in a way he's never attacked before. There will always be tests, but I believe the enemy has kicked it up a notch. It seems as if there has been a testing time as never before.

I know that in the recent past, RHEMA, as well as our family personally, has encountered many tests. First, my father passed away. I was daddy's girl, and losing my daddy was a hard time in my life. Then there was battle after battle after battle. I've seen testings before, but I had never seen anything like these recent battles.

It seemed when we turned to the right, there was something "slapping us in the face." When we turned to the left, there was something else there "slapping us in the face." If we turned forward, thinking we would march away from the battles, there was something there. If we turned in the opposite direction—bam!—there was something there too! They were not just battles; this was all-out war!

Then the devil tried to land a final blow with the death of my father-in-law in September 2003. But RHEMA will keep going till Jesus comes! We have taken up the torch and banner—the fires of the Spirit and the banner of faith in God's Word—and we will continue to fulfill the vision and the plan God gave so many years ago.

I thank God for the foundation I had in Him. I knew my hope was built on the Solid Rock, the Lord Jesus Christ. I knew I was committed to complete the plan of God for my life. Regardless of what might come or what might go, I was going to keep my focus on Jesus.

We Must Not Waver!

It's important to remember during the proving season that we don't wrestle against flesh and blood, but against principalities and powers of darkness (Eph. 6:12). The thing that kept me going—and what will keep you going—is knowing that God is on our side. He will never let us down. He will always see us through.

One of the most important things to remember is this: We must not waver! We must never question God, asking, "Why?" or blame God for the attacks of the enemy. There will be tests in life, but God is the One who helps us overcome!

One thing my father-in-law always taught us was to not get into the arena of questioning. He always encouraged us to trust God. God is faithful and will fulfill His promises.

The Lord is stretching us because we have a mighty work to do in these last days. It is a work such as we've not seen before. And it's important that we rise to the occasion and commit to the cause.

As we go through tests and trials and come through victorious, we will stand stronger than ever before. No matter what comes our way, as long as we stand on the Rock of Christ Jesus, we cannot go under for going over!

You may be walking through a valley right now, but don't camp in it. Keep walking through to the other side. On the other side is your victory, your peace, and the grace you need to fulfill the assignment God has for you.

You may have gone through a lot of battles in the past, or you may still be going through some right now, but know that the enemy always attacks those for whom God has great assignments. So if you've been attacked fiercely, know that you must have a big assignment!

The following is a prophetic utterance I received from the Lord as I ministered at a *Kindle the Flame* Women's Conference along these same lines. I believe it applies to all of us today.

And we shall run the race.

And we shall walk the course.

And we shall go forth for the plan of God for our life.

And we shall not be deterred.

Oh no, no, no, no, no!

But we shall walk forward—

Forward, forward, forward, not looking to the right,

Not looking to the left,

Not paying attention to the circumstances on either side.

But we shall march to the heartbeat of God.

And those orders shall come very strongly.

And those orders shall come very clearly.

And we shall not question.

No, no, no, no, no, no, no! We shall not question.

But we shall go forth with our assignment.

*For there are many assignments that must be
accomplished.*

And as we join together in one mind and one accord,

Oh, yes, there shall be a manifestation as never before.

Many miracles, many miracles shall come to pass,

A mighty outpouring of My Spirit.

But you must lay aside every weight.

Yes! Every weight!

And as you lay aside those weights,

I'll be able to use you.

You've cried out, "Lord, use me! Use me! Use me!"

Lay aside those weights.

Lay aside those things that hinder.

For I have called you. Yes, I have.

But you must lay aside those weights.

And as you do, the assignment is great.

Yes, the assignment is great!

And much fruit, much fruit, shall come to pass.

God is calling for commitment, and we must be serious about our commitment to Him. Time is short, for I believe that we are living in the last days. There's a great work for all of us to do. There's a great work for men, women, children, and teenagers. We all have our part, so we must gather the forces and work together to fulfill the plan.

✓It's not always easy to fulfill God's plan for our life. His plan is not always what we want to do. You may have been in turmoil for many years because God has spoken to you and asked you to do certain things, but you've refused to do them.

Perhaps you have held grudges for years, even when God has asked you to forgive. As you continue to hold that grudge, the Lord is saying, "Forgive. You need to forgive."

You may have been living with hurts for years—hurts from childhood, bad memories that keep coming to you. Those memories have been like a wall in front of you. You haven't been able to progress because of those haunting memories. The Lord wants to erase those memories today. He wants to set you free. You will no longer be bound by those, because the Lord is going to give you "spiritual amnesia" as you obey Him!

If you have been living with painful memories from the past, make a quality decision that you will not allow the enemy to bring those memories back to you. He has haunted you for years and years, and the hurt in your life has hindered you in relationships. But you can receive healing if you'll let the healing balm of the Holy Spirit bathe you and wash those wounds away.

God wants to take us all higher. He wants to take us deeper as we bask in His Presence and say, "Not our will, Father, but Your will be done." It's so important to follow the perfect plan of God for our life!

I'm committed to following His plan. Are you ready to make that commitment? Are you ready to humble yourself in the season of preparation and allow God to mold you, shape you, and "season" you? Are you ready to be patient in the waiting season and to rest in the Lord, waiting for His timing? Are you ready to stand strong during the season of proving and to refuse to waver as you remain faithful to God's call, no matter what comes your way?

CHAPTER 4

Thank God for the Holy Ghost!

You may wonder if you have what it takes to answer yes to these questions: Are you ready to commit wholeheartedly to the Lord? Are you ready to humble yourself before Him? Are you ready to be patient and to stand strong until He brings His plan to pass in your life?

The truth is, in and of yourself, you *can't* answer yes. You need the power and Presence of the Holy Spirit in order to accomplish God's plan.

You don't know what lies ahead of you; it's impossible for you to know all that the future holds. As I've said, for years I didn't know how God's plan for my life would unfold. Thank God, He keeps some of His secrets for a *long* time! If I had known from day one all that God had planned for me, I would have been trembling in my boots and probably would have quit before I ever started.

You don't need to know how every detail of God's plan for your life will take place. You just need to trust Him and follow the Holy Spirit as He leads and guides you along life's path. Remember what Paul said in Acts chapter 20, not knowing what his future held, but trusting in the One who held his future.

ACTS 20:22-24 (*Amplified*)

22 And now, you see, I am going to Jerusalem, bound by the [Holy] Spirit and obligated and compelled by the [convictions of my own] spirit, not knowing what will befall me there—

23 Except that the Holy Spirit clearly and emphatically affirms to me in city after city that imprisonment and suffering await me.

24 But none of these things move me; neither do I esteem my life dear to myself, if only I may finish my course with joy and the ministry which I have obtained from [which was entrusted to me by] the Lord Jesus, faithfully to attest to the good news (Gospel) of God's

grace (His unmerited favor, spiritual bless-ing, and mercy).

The Apostle Paul said, "I don't know what lies before me. I don't know what might befall me. All I know is that I am bound by the Holy Spirit and obligated and com-pelled by the convictions of my own spirit." Paul followed the leading of the Holy Spirit, knowing that his obedience would enable him to finish his course with joy.

✓Rely on the Holy Ghost

It's important to always follow and obey what the Holy Ghost is leading you to do. Whatever lies before you, whatever your course in life, rest assured that if you follow the Holy Spirit, you *shall* finish your course with joy!

If you will obey the Holy Spirit, He will lead you and guide you. He will be your Comforter and Helper if you'll look to the Greater One Who is inside you. The Holy Ghost will be your *Counselor*. What are you going to do when you don't know what to do? You're going to rely on the Holy Spirit, the Counselor, for counsel and help. The Holy Ghost is also your *Intercessor*, your *Advocate*, your *Standby,* and your *Strengthener* (John 14:26 *Amplified*). When you think you can't go any further, call upon the Holy

Spirit to be your Strengthener. He will quicken, or make alive, and strengthen your mortal body (Rom. 8:11).

The Holy Ghost will also bring things to our remembrance. John 14:26 says, *"But the Comforter, which is the Holy Ghost, whom the Father will send in my name, he shall teach you all things, and bring all things to your remembrance, whatsoever I have said unto you."* Now don't misunderstand me, students cannot ask the Holy Spirit to bring something to their remembrance that they never studied and learned in the first place.

My mother taught me this scripture when I was very young. And, boy, did I study! And even from the time I was in the first grade, I was taught to pray before I took a test. My mother told me, "You've studied. Now pray and ask the Holy Spirit to bring those things you learned to your remembrance." I did what she taught me. I called upon the Holy Spirit, and He accommodated me. Not to brag on myself, but to brag on God, when I graduated from high school, I had the second highest grade point average in a class of 400 people.

The Holy Spirit will bring things to your remembrance. He will also teach you all things and show you things to come (John 16:13). There's no way you can see into the future and prepare for everything you will ever encounter in life. So what should you do? You should call upon the Holy Spirit. Rely on the One who lives inside you, because He is the Great Teacher.

LUKE 12:12

✓ **12 For the Holy Ghost shall teach you in the same hour what ye ought to say.**

Many times, the apostles found themselves in positions in which they needed an answer quickly! Whether testifying or witnessing or being accused, they needed to know what to say. And the Holy Ghost gave them the right words.

There may be times in life that you must make a split-second decision. It may be a life-or-death decision, but if you will call upon the Greater One inside you, He will tell you what to do. He will teach you what to say. The Holy Ghost will be your Helper, your Strengthener, and your Standby—He's standing by waiting to help you!

JOHN 14:26 (*Amplified*)

26 But the Comforter (Counselor, Helper, Intercessor, Advocate, Strengthener, Standby), the Holy Spirit, Whom the Father will send in My name [in My place, to represent Me and act on My behalf], He will teach you all things. And He will cause you to recall (will remind

you of, bring to your remembrance) everything I have told you.

As you rely on the Holy Ghost, determined to follow God's plan for your life, you will be able to finish your course with joy (Acts 20:24). You will be able to echo what the Apostle Paul said, "I have fought the good fight, finished the race, and kept the faith" (2 Tim. 4:7).

The Great Teacher, the Holy Spirit, can teach us everything we need to know to fight the good fight of faith and to finish our race victoriously. But we must invite Him to teach us and welcome His Presence. It is the anointing that breaks the yoke (Isa. 10:27), and there is nothing like the Presence of God—the anointing or power of God!

I love being in God's Presence. There is no other place I would rather be. His Presence is what I seek most in my life. My prayer is, "God, I want to know more of You. I want to be more like You." And that should be your prayer too.

For more than 30 years, my husband and I and all who have labored with us have been laying a foundation for RHEMA Bible Training Center. We have more than 28,000 graduates, and I'm grateful for all that we've accomplished for and with the Lord. But I remember well that first year of school. It was a hard, hard year in the natural. We would never have made it through without the Holy Ghost and His power at work on our behalf.

In the years that have followed, it seems anything that could be shaken has been shaken. There have been times in the natural that my husband and I had to remember our decision that we would keep RHEMA Bible Training Center going no matter what. Daily we prayed the finances in—sometimes not knowing how we were going to pay the bills the next day.

We believed God on a daily basis with all the faith we had, and daily we saw God come through. He never was early; and sometimes we thought He was going to be late! But He was always right on time. Sometimes the timing didn't seem right on time to us, but God's timing is not always our timing.

At times we have to fight battles in order to reach the new level to which God wants to take us. Perhaps you have been fighting battles for quite some time. In your mind, you may not be able to see how God is going to turn your situation around for your good. You may be asking, "How, God, will this work out for me?"

Stand and see the salvation of the Lord (*see* 2 Chron. 20:17)! Watch Him as He works on your behalf. The road to fulfilling His plan for your life isn't always easy. But He is calling you. Yes, there will be tests and trials. Will you be faithful to the call? Those who are faithful and those who are committed shall witness a glory that has not been seen before—a glory indescribable in human language.

Yield to the Lord's calling. Be committed to His call upon your life. Walk with Him, and He will teach you what you need to know in order to accomplish His plan for you. You will experience a great victory in the battles you have been fighting. Be strong and courageous and keep fighting the good fight of faith (1 Tim. 6:12).

I encourage you to stay prayed up. Stay sensitive to the Holy Spirit's leading. Opportunities will come to you. And in the meantime, you are being prepared for your calling. So lay aside every weight that could easily beset you and hinder you from fulfilling your calling and winning your race (Heb. 12:1).

You see, there are not only sins, but there are weights. Those weights will distract you from your mission, so lay aside those things. They may not be sins or things that will prevent you from going to Heaven. But they will keep you from fulfilling your divine purpose. Distractions are part of the enemy's device. He uses distractions to try to keep you from walking in God's divine purpose. So lay aside those weights!

Go before the Lord; seek His face, listen to His voice, and He will speak to you strongly and clearly. As part of the preparation for your calling, He will teach you how to hear His voice.

In order to accurately follow God's plan for your life, you have to be able to understand the directions or instructions He gives you. You have to clearly see that which He has ordained you to do. And you must be divinely led by Him. When the Lord leads you, there is divine protection, divine guidance, and divine wisdom.

As you seek His face, you will be emboldened as never before. When you know what He's called you to do, there is a boldness that accompanies His calling. As you yield to that boldness, doors will open for you. You will have more opportunities and supernatural favor than you can fathom. Oh, the plans God has for you are far greater than those which you have imagined for yourself!

Be faithful to pass each test that is set before you. Remember, you can't go to the next part of God's plan until you successfully complete what He has set before you. Just as in school when you couldn't go to the next grade until you first passed the grade you were in, you must pass each test in your spiritual walk. You must stay faithful and committed to walking one step at a time. As you do, only time and eternity will tell all the great things that will be accomplished through you and by you.

A Good Idea May Not Be God's Idea

Some seemingly good opportunities may come your way that are not of God, and it will be easy to say yes to them. But if you're not careful, you will say yes to something that is good but not of God. The devil would love more than anything to get us off course, so we must learn to be sensitive to the Holy Spirit's leading in order to discern which opportunities are from God and truly good for us and which ones are distractions.

I remember one time quite well when the enemy tried to use his distraction tactic on my husband and me. To make a long story short, my husband had just left the Armed Forces. We were newly married and going into ministry.

My husband was ready to preach the Gospel to the world, but there were few preaching opportunities to be had. Without opportunities, there was no money. And without money, there was nothing to live on except what I was earning—an income of $50 a week.

Those are the moments the enemy loves to seize upon. He comes to each of us when we're down or when life looks bleak and tries to take advantage of the situation. But he doesn't always come in obvious ways. Sometimes he subtly uses the distraction tactic.

The enemy came to my husband with a seemingly wonderful opportunity from the U.S. government. The opportunity seemed wonderful in the natural because it solved Ken's immediate problems of his not having a job and not bringing in any income. But it wasn't truly wonderful, because it would have taken us out of God's plan for our life.

At the time, I had a regular job making $50 a week. Ken's speaking engagements were few and far between, so we were living on my income. Of course, the enemy screamed in Ken's ears, "You're not providing for your new bride. You need to get a job and be a better husband."

I was at work when Ken received a telegram from the government offering him a job that paid $15,000 a year. Back then that was a lot of money, and it sounded even better when we were making only $200 a month! When I came home from work that day, Ken was so excited because he was going to be able to provide for us handsomely. But I wasn't about to be bought by the enemy's money. As Ken told me about the opportunity, I became gripped on the inside by the power of God—by the Holy Ghost.

Hey, God, Why Is It Taking So Long?

A supernatural boldness began to rise up in me, reminding me that from the age of nine, I had known I was called to the ministry and to stand by my husband in ministry. I knew Ken was called to the ministry. Knowing the importance of staying in the will of God, I became frightened by this opportunity. A person can have all the world's goods and all the money he desires, but if he's not in God's will, all that he has is good for nothing.

As a new bride, I had been taught to honor and respect my husband. I knew Ken was excited about the job out of a pure motive and desire to provide for me! But I was so gripped by this boldness, I wasn't going to stand for it! I refused to be deterred by any amount of money or any job offer.

At that early point in our marriage, I had not developed my communication skills very well. I only knew one way to convey the strong stirring on the inside of me and I said to Ken, "I want to tell you what! I married a preacher, and I intend on living with a preacher!" Then I ran out the door and slammed it behind me!

I trusted that God would talk to Ken, and I trusted that Ken would let me back in the door! Thank the Lord for a husband who knows the voice of God. The Lord did speak to Ken, and he turned the job down. As they say, the rest is history.

I am sharing this with you to show you how the enemy will try to twist things. In our situation, the devil even brought a scriptural principle into play, telling Ken that he wasn't any good because he wasn't providing for his household (1 Tim. 5:8). But, thankfully, we didn't fall for the devil's distraction. We remained committed to God's plan for our life and we followed the Holy Spirit's leading every step of the way. He kept us from getting distracted. He kept us on course, and He will do the same for you!

Be Faithful—Be Blessed

It wasn't fun living on $50 a week. But it was a time of commitment, preparation, waiting, and proving. Someone might think everything fell into place for us quickly. No, no, no! Over the next several years, every time we stepped into another ministry opportunity we knew God had designed for us, our salary was cut in half!

But we knew we were in God's perfect will. We may not have had everything we had thought we would have, but we didn't go hungry, and we always had clothes on our back. And we were happy because we were fulfilling the plan of God for our life.

And I believe that the life we are living now—a life of blessings and ministry beyond our imagination—would not have happened if we had not walked in the will of God all along. Back when we turned down the government job for those few-and-far-between ministry opportunities, we didn't know that we would one day be teaching tens of thousands of students who would go all over the world preaching the Gospel.

We had no idea of the scope and magnitude of God's plan. But we stayed faithful each step of the way. We never desired or hoped to do what we are doing now. We didn't pray and believe God for it. We simply said, "God, we want to walk in Your ways and in Your plan. More than anything else in life, we want to be obedient to Your call." What if we had not surrendered to God's will? Would RHEMA Bible Training Center be what it is today?

And I ask you the same question: What if *you* don't surrender to God's will? What will happen if *you* don't fulfill *your* great destiny?

I'm so thankful that I yielded to the call. I'm so thankful that I said yes. One reason is because I can lie down at night in peace. When you're not walking in the will of God, there is no peace!

Yes, there will always be trials and circumstances and problems that come our way, even while we're in the perfect will of God. But we can lie down at night, saying, "God, I'm doing what You've asked me to do. So I know

You will take care of me and cause everything to work out for my good [Rom. 8:28]. I can walk in peace and victory, knowing that You are going to carry me through to the other side."

The enemy will come to you and try to take advantage of any weaknesses he can seize upon. He will try to deter you from your call. He will try to tempt you, and your carnal man will try to rise up (1 Cor. 2:14; 3:1). The lust of the flesh will try to rise up (Rom. 8:5–6). We're all human. We all have to learn to resist temptation. When those moments come, what do we do? *Flee youthful lusts!* (*See* 2 Tim. 2:22.) We are to slap the devil in the face, so to speak, and say, "Devil, you will not deter me from finishing my course. No, no, no! I started this course with the intention of finishing it, and with God's help, I will do just that!"

Finish What You've Started

My parents always told me, "Never start anything you don't intend to finish." If I ever joined a club or activity and in the middle of participating realized that it wasn't what I wanted to do, it was just too bad. My parents made me finish the term or season to which I had committed.

I'm so thankful my parents taught me the principle of finishing what I started. It's a godly principle of faithfulness and commitment that we can all benefit from practicing.

God did not call you to have you give up and quit before finishing your course. So when those times come (and *they will come*) when you feel like giving up, just look the devil square in the face and say, "Mr. Devil, I am going to finish my course! I'm going to fulfill the call of God on my life!"

God rewards the faithful. So remember your call and the plan of God for your life. Just as the Apostle Paul did, forget what is behind and "strain" toward what is ahead. Focus your eyes on winning the prize.

PHILIPPIANS 3:12–14 (*NIV*)

12 Not that I have already obtained all this, or have already been made perfect, but I press on to take hold of that for which Christ Jesus took hold of me.

13 Brothers, I do not consider myself yet to have taken hold of it. But one thing I do: Forgetting what is behind and straining toward what is ahead,

14 I press on toward the goal to win the prize for which God has called me heavenward in Christ Jesus.

In order to win the prize, you must be trained well. You must be sharp, for the work that God has for you to do is specialized. You have to be trained for it. Therefore, now is the time to focus.

I'm excited about what God has in store for all of us. I believe we're going to go to higher heights and deeper depths. God wants to move each of us into a closer relationship with Him. He wants us to get to the point where we are walking in the Spirit every moment of our life.

It's important to stay in the Spirit every minute of your life. Even though your life may be busy and time may be short, that doesn't mean you can neglect your prayer life. Pray continually in the Spirit, building yourself up on your most holy faith (Jude 20).

Walking in the Spirit does not mean that you are flaky in the Spirit. There's a big difference. One of the reasons it took me so long to obey God about holding a women's conference is because I'd seen so many women act superficial and blame it on the Spirit! I didn't want to be a part of any flakiness. So I wrestled for many years with God about His plan for me, hoping I could change His mind. But we don't change God's mind too often, do we?

Leaning on the Arm of the Spirit

I finally said, "Okay, God. I'll do it. But You know I can't do anything in the natural. I'm going to have to depend wholly upon the Holy Ghost. And the one thing that I must know is that You're going to meet me with Your anointing." I did, and He did!

Yes, I've stepped into my place—slowly but willingly. And we must all step into our place, because it's going to take all of us in our place working together to bring to pass the plan of God for this last hour.

Just as God has stretched me and turned me every which way but loose, He's going to do the same for you. God is going to stretch you from now until the end of your life. Let Him stretch you. You'll walk in peace. You'll walk in prosperity. You'll walk in health. And you'll walk in victory. Are you ready to walk in those places? Are you ready to accept your call?

When I asked the Lord, "Why do You always ask me to do something I don't feel comfortable doing?" He said, "Lynette, I want you to learn to wholly depend upon Me!" We all must come to the place where we say, "God, I am totally depending upon You. All that I am, all that I have, and all that I am capable of doing is found only in You."

There is supernatural ability and grace found in the Presence of God. The Holy Spirit has been given to us and wants to empower us and enable us to walk out God's plan. But we must wholly depend upon Him. As we do, we will experience much peace and joy *and* walk in victory in every area of life.

CHAPTER 5

'I Am Determined!'

We must commit to God's plan and prepare ourselves so that we are ready to accomplish what God has for us. We must hold steady through seasons of waiting and through the proving seasons. Throughout every season of life, we must remain determined that we will go on with God—no matter what.

Paul said in First Corinthians 2:2, *"For I determined not to know any thing among you, save Jesus Christ, and him crucified."*

It is vitally important that we become firmly established in Jesus Christ and Him crucified. We must determine that we won't allow anything or anyone to distract us or become more important to us than Jesus.

In Paul's day, the Jews wanted a sign before they would believe (1 Cor. 1:22). That is not so different from people today. Most people want physical proof before they will believe. In Paul's day, the Greeks wanted wisdom before they would believe (1 Cor. 1:22). That's typical of today too. Many people want scientific or intellectual proof before they will believe.

But Paul told the people plainly and in no uncertain terms that he was not going to be diverted by the people's desire for mere sensation. He told them to fix their eyes firmly on the fact of Christ and Him crucified.

Paul said, "I'm not going to get involved in controversial teachings or trivial doctrinal disputes. I'm going to keep my eyes on the One Who will keep me going. When the storms of life are raging, I can keep my eyes on the One Who was crucified and raised from the dead—the One Who will bring me through anything I may encounter!"

We must be equally determined to fix our eyes upon Jesus and Him only. We're not going to veer to the right; we're not going to veer to the left. We're going to build a foundation that nothing can shake! Whatever may come our way, we will be standing *firmly* on the Rock of the Lord Jesus Christ. He will carry us through every circumstance we face in life. And when we meet the devil head on, we can boldly say to him, "I am determined!"

Whether or not you realize it, when you go to church or to special meetings, you are in a spiritual incubator. In other words, you are surrounded by other Christians who will join their faith with yours. You are under a corporate anointing in which wonderful things can take place. You are embraced by people who love you and are concerned about you and want to see you do well in life. In that kind of atmosphere, it is easy to get excited about commitment. It's easy to believe that you will stay determined no matter what. In a church service, you can feel so good that it's easy to feel invincible.

But let me warn you, as soon as you are thrust out into the world, the devil would love to just smack you right in the face! He would love to try to throw something your way just to see if you really believe what you say you believe. It's as if he's saying, "Let's see what kind of foundation you have. Let's see how committed you really are. Let's see if I can get you off your course."

The devil loves to cause Christians to fall, and he usually doesn't attack them when they're in church. When the attacks do come, that's when you've got to reach way down inside and say, "Devil, let me tell you a thing or two! I've made up my mind! I am determined to go on with God!"

You may have been running from God's call for a long time and have been miserable for years. It's time to say,

"Yes, Lord, I'll commit. I'll obey. I'll do what You've asked me to do—what You've been calling me to do for years." It's important to settle the issue right now, before you are in the midst of an attack.

But commitment doesn't end when you say yes to the Lord. That's only the *beginning* of commitment. Commitment is tested by fire. First Peter 1:7 says, *"That the trial of your faith, being much more precious than of gold that perisheth, though it be tried with fire, might be found unto praise and honour and glory at the appearing of Jesus Christ."*

Refined by Fire

I remember going to a gold mine when I was visiting South Africa. Gold is a precious and valuable metal, but in its natural state, gold contains many impurities. Before gold can be used, the impurities are removed—by fire.

While on this trip, I watched as gold was placed into a crucible (a heat-resistant container in which metals are melted) and fired to the point that it became liquid. While the gold was in this liquid form, the impurities once buried deep within the gold rose to the top of the crucible. After the impurities were removed, the remaining liquid was cooled to reveal a pure, beautiful gold.

Other definitions for "crucible" include *a severe trial or ordeal; testing circumstances; a place or set of circumstances where people or things are subjected to forces that test them and often make them change.* Sometimes we may be placed in the crucible of life. And we may feel like we are being burned with fire. But as those tests heat us, we must allow God to remove the impurities from our life. Then all that will remain is beautiful gold.

When the trials of life come to you, rejoice knowing that while you are being tested by fire, you are also being purified and made into something beautiful that God can use. So remain determined to make it through the fire. Make up your mind right now that you will persevere so that when life throws something your way, you are undaunted. When the devil tries to make you doubt your calling, you can boldly say to him, "Devil, it's already settled! I am determined to make it through. I'm going to hold out to the end."

Compromise Is Not an Option

You have to be as determined as Daniel was in the Old Testament. Nothing was going to stop him from serving his God. Daniel did not compromise—even in the face of enormous pressure.

Hey, God, Why Is It Taking So Long?

One problem with Christians today is that there is too much compromise taking place. In fact, some believers have compromised so much that you can't tell the difference between them and non-Christians. That's a sad indictment. We must become determined to never compromise our convictions.

Daniel was a captive in a foreign land when his godly actions won the attention of the king. Daniel 6:3 says, "Now Daniel so distinguished himself among the administrators and the satraps by his exceptional qualities that the king planned to set him over the whole kingdom" (*NIV*). Daniel's favor and position with the king made the other leaders in the kingdom jealous, so they tried to find charges against Daniel. Verse 4 says, "They were unable to do so. They could find no corruption in him, because he was trustworthy and neither corrupt nor negligent" (*NIV*). So these jealous leaders conspired to attack Daniel's faith in God.

DANIEL 6:5–15 (*NIV*)

5 Finally these men said, "We will never find any basis for charges against this man Daniel unless it has something to do with the law of his God."

6 So the administrators and the satraps went as a group to the king and said: "O King Darius, live for ever!

7 The royal administrators, prefects, satraps, advisers and governors have all agreed that the king should issue an edict and enforce the decree that anyone who prays to any god or man during the next thirty days, except to you, O king, shall be thrown into the lions' den.

8 Now, O king, issue the decree and put it in writing so that it cannot be altered—in accordance with the laws of the Medes and Persians, which cannot be repealed."

9 So King Darius put the decree in writing.

10 Now when Daniel learned that the decree had been published, he went home to his upstairs room where the windows opened toward Jerusalem. Three times a day he got down on his knees and prayed, giving thanks to his God, JUST AS HE HAD DONE BEFORE.

11 Then these men went as a group and found Daniel praying and asking God for help.

12 So they went to the king and spoke to him about his royal decree: "Did you not publish a decree that during the next thirty days anyone who prays to any god or man except to you, O king, would be thrown into the lions' den?" The king answered, "The decree stands—in accordance with the laws of the Medes and Persians, which cannot be repealed."

13 Then they said to the king, "Daniel, who is one of the exiles from Judah, pays no attention to you, O king, or to the decree you put in writing. He still prays three times a day."

14 When the king heard this, he was greatly distressed; he was determined to rescue Daniel and made every effort until sundown to save him.

15 Then the men went as a group to the king and said to him, "Remember, O king, that according to the law of the Medes and Persians no decree or edict that the king issues can be changed."

When the decree was made that no one was to pray to any god or to anyone except the king, what did Daniel do?

Did he stop serving the Lord or hide away to serve Him secretly in fear of being caught? No. Daniel did not compromise at all. He went up to his house. He opened his windows. He knelt down for all to see and prayed to his God—the God he knew would deliver him out of every test and trouble.

Daniel was determined that he would not compromise. He was confident of the fact that his God was able to deliver him out of any situation. Not only was *Daniel* convinced that his God was able to deliver him from the consequences of his actions, but he had lived such a life in front of the king that the *king* believed Daniel's God could deliver him. Even as the king placed Daniel in the lions' den, he said, *"Thy God whom thou servest CONTINUALLY, he will deliver thee"* (Dan. 6:16).

Daniel had served God so faithfully that even the king was confident that God would deliver him. The problem some Christians have today is that they don't serve God faithfully or *continually*. Their relationship with God is so up and down that it's hard for them to expect God to deliver them.

Confidence in the Midst of the Fire

We need to have such a consistent and continual relationship with God that we are able to establish a firm foundation in the Word.

Hey, God, Why Is It Taking So Long?

Not only do we need to be as faithful and determined as Daniel, knowing that our God will deliver us out of every trial, but we also need to be as committed as the three Hebrew young men, Shadrach, Meshach, and Abednego. These young men were determined that they would not bow before the king's graven image. And when they were told they would be thrown into a fiery furnace for their refusal, they did not compromise.

DANIEL 3:12–18

12 There are certain Jews whom thou hast set over the affairs of the province of Babylon, Shadrach, Meshach, and Abednego; these men, O king, have not regarded thee: they serve not thy gods, nor worship the golden image which thou hast set up.

13 Then Nebuchadnezzar in his rage and fury commanded to bring Shadrach, Meshach, and Abednego. Then they brought these men before the king.

14 Nebuchadnezzar spake and said unto them, Is it true, O Shadrach, Meshach, and Abednego, do not ye serve my gods, nor worship the golden image which I have set up?
15 Now if ye be ready that at what time ye hear

the sound of the cornet, flute, harp, sackbut, psaltery, and dulcimer, and all kinds of musick, ye fall down and worship the image which I have made; well: but if ye worship not, ye shall be cast the same hour into the midst of a burning fiery furnace; and who is that God that shall deliver you out of my hands?

16 Shadrach, Meshach, and Abednego, answered and said to the king, O Nebuchadnezzar, we are not careful to answer thee in this matter.

17 If it be so, our God whom we serve is able to deliver us from the burning fiery furnace, and he will deliver us out of thine hand, O king.

18 But if not, be it known unto thee, O king, that we will not serve thy gods, nor worship the golden image which thou hast set up.

When asked by the king what god was able to deliver them out of his hands, Shadrach, Meshach, and Abednego said, "We're not careful to answer you in this matter." In other words, they said, "We don't have to think about your question; we can answer you immediately." And answer him they did! They said, ". . . OUR GOD WHOM WE SERVE *is able to deliver us from the burning fiery furnace, and he will deliver us out of thine hand, O king"* (v. 17).

Our foundation should be so firmly fixed on the Word of God that we don't have to think but can answer immediately when asked who is able to deliver us. We should have the same faith and confidence that Shadrach, Meshach, and Abednego had in the Lord.

The Inseparable Mix of Faith and Commitment

Not only did Shadrach, Meshach, and Abednego have faith, but they were committed to that faith, no matter what. You see, it was a statement of their faith when they said, "If you throw us into the fire, our God Whom we serve is able to deliver us from the fiery furnace and will deliver us out of your hand." Then they followed their statement of faith by stating their commitment: *"But if not, be it known unto thee, O king, that we will not serve thy gods, nor worship the golden image which thou hast set up"* (v. 18).

Their faith was exhibited in their belief that God was going to deliver them out of the fire. But their commitment to God was so strong that even if He *didn't* deliver them, Shadrach, Meshach, and Abednego still wouldn't compromise and bow to the idol. They were going to continue to serve the Lord their God, no matter what.

Friend, it takes that kind of commitment to live a godly life in this world. Yes, it's very important to have faith. But you not only need faith, you need commitment. You must be as committed as Daniel, Shadrach, Meshach, and Abednego. You must be determined to live for God, even if you are the only one doing so. You must be determined to remain faithful to God without compromise.

Life Is an Opportunity to Triumph

One person who was pressured on all sides to give up the faith was the Apostle Paul. Yet, he was determined to fulfill God's plan for his life. In Acts 20:23 and 24, he said, "I only know that in every city the Holy Spirit warns me that prison and hardships are facing me. However, I consider my life worth nothing to me, if only I may finish the race and complete the task the Lord Jesus has given me—the task of testifying to the gospel of God's grace" (NIV).

Too many times, we think that if we have accepted God's call and are following His plan, life will be a bed of roses. That's simply not the case. Look at everything Paul went through while following God's plan!

2 CORINTHIANS 11:25–28

25 Thrice was I beaten with rods, once was I stoned, thrice I suffered shipwreck, a night and a day I have been in the deep;

26 In journeyings often, in perils of waters, in perils of robbers, in perils by mine own countrymen, in perils by the heathen, in perils in the city, in perils in the wilderness, in perils in the sea, in perils among false brethren;

27 In weariness and painfulness, in watchings often, in hunger and thirst, in fastings often, in cold and nakedness.

28 Beside those things that are without, that which cometh upon me daily, the care of all the churches.

Paul faced various perils and afflictions all the time. He had to be extremely committed and determined to press through the many obstacles that tried to keep him from fulfilling God's plan. In Second Corinthians 2:14, Paul tells us the reason he was able to persevere: *"Now thanks be unto God, which always causeth us to triumph in Christ, and maketh manifest the savour of his knowledge by us in every place."*

In the midst of adverse circumstances we, too, can boldly say, "Thanks be to God, who always causes us to triumph in Christ Jesus!" But we must be as committed as Paul was. In other words, it's easy to quote Second Corinthians 2:14 when everything in life is going well. But can we say it and believe it, even when circumstances are against us? Can we say as Paul did, *"Therefore I take pleasure in infirmities, in reproaches, in necessities, in persecutions, in distresses for Christ's sake: for when I am weak, then am I strong"* (2 Cor. 12:10)? Do we have the confidence to say that God *always* causes us to triumph, even when we are being beaten for preaching the Gospel?

While you may never have been *physically* beaten, you may feel beaten by the attacks of the enemy. You may feel beaten in your finances, in your health, or in the health of your children or family. There may be other circumstances that have tried to beat you down. When the opportunities to feel beaten come your way, take a stand and say, "No, devil! I'll not take that opportunity. I refuse this in the Name of Jesus. You may be trying to beat me down, but I always triumph in Christ Jesus!"

If you are feeling beaten in your finances, tell the devil to take his hands off your finances. Command the ministering spirits to go and cause your money to come to you, because Philippians 4:19 says your God shall supply all your needs according to His riches in glory!

If you are feeling beaten in your physical body, you can say to the devil, "I'll not take your opportunity of sickness. I'll not accept that opportunity, for First Peter 2:24 says I was healed by the stripes Jesus bore. And if I *was* healed, then I *am* healed!"

No Trespassing!

If you're feeling pain in your body right now, take God's promises. Take them right now and be healed in the Name of Jesus. Say to the enemy, "I'll not accept your sickness package. I have a better opportunity! I've been offered the *healing* package! And it's greater than your package.

"Satan, I'm posting a 'No Trespassing' sign. I am God's property, and you can no longer trespass here. You must leave my health alone. You must leave my house alone. You must leave my family alone. You are not allowed access into my life!"

The enemy likes to attack our family. He knows if he can attack our children, he can really get to us. When my children were attacked with sickness, my husband and I firmly said, "Satan, we've posted 'No Trespassing' signs. Now we command you in the Name of Jesus to get out of here, because you are trespassing on God's property!"

If you have to, just take your foot and kick the devil out the door of your house! Don't yell and scream at your spouse—scream at the devil! Sometimes I think Satan is hard of hearing, so I *yell*, "Satan, in the Name of Jesus, *GET OUT OF HERE!* I'm not going to put up with your foolishness any longer!"

Post your "No Trespassing" signs. Be determined and committed. Refuse to compromise or to quit. Satan won't hang around for very long when he realizes you mean business. He knows when he's been defeated. He knows when you are determined to fight the good fight of faith!

The devil will hang around as long as you let him. It's up to you to put him on the run. One of the best ways to put the devil on the run is by speaking the Name of Jesus. Many times when storms have raged all around me, I would just lift my eyes to the heavens and said, "Jesus. Jesus. Jesus." As I spoke His Name, peace began to come.

Isaiah 26:3 says, *"Thou wilt keep him in perfect peace, whose mind is stayed on thee: because he trusteth in thee."* When you don't have peace, and storms are raging all around you, close your eyes. Lift your face to the heavens and speak the Name of Jesus until you find peace in the midst of the storm.

There Is Power in the Word

There's power in the Name of Jesus, and there is power in the Word of God. When my faith and my determination seem to be wavering, I start quoting the Word, because fear is dispelled by faith. And where does faith come? *"So then faith cometh by hearing, and hearing by the word of God"* (Rom. 10:17).

I quote the Word so I can *hear* the Word of God. Sometimes you need to read the Bible out loud. Don't just read it silently; speak it so your ears can hear you saying it. When King David was greatly distressed, he *encouraged himself* in the Lord (1 Sam. 30:6). When you don't have anyone else to build you up, speak the Word of God and encouragement will come every time.

There have been many times in my life when I didn't *feel* like I had the victory. Many times I have gone to a church service when I didn't feel like going. The cares of life were getting to me, and I didn't feel like seeing one more person. I didn't want to smile again. I was tired of smiling.

But every time I felt that way, someone in the service would unknowingly minister to me and my situation. Sometimes it was the worship songs that were sung. They would minister to my heart and build me up in faith. Many times as the associate pastors made the announcements, the Spirit of God came upon them and they ministered words meant just for me.

Of course, they didn't know they were ministering to me. No one knew in those times that *I* needed to be ministered to. Even though I'm in the ministry, there are times I need ministry too. And through the worship, exhortation, or sermon, I received help in my time of need because I was hearing the Word of God.

Speak the Word When You Don't Feel Like Talking

It's so important to speak the Word. It lifts our faith and strengthens our heart. I made myself go to those services even when I didn't feel like going, and after hearing the Word, I left those services on cloud nine. Too many times we allow ourselves to throw a pity party, and we go hide in the corner when we don't feel like seeing anyone.

We know the Word, but we don't want to speak it. We just want to have a pity party. And the devil has a heyday. Determine in your heart right now that you're not going to have a pity party, regardless of what comes your way.

When you get discouraged, speak the Word. When you need finances, speak the Word. When you're sick, speak the Word. And I guarantee you, as you speak the

Word, those confessions of faith will become realities in your life.

Fight the Fight and Finish Your Course

As Paul admonished Timothy, I admonish you: Determine in your heart right now that you will fight the good fight, finish your course, and keep the faith.

2 TIMOTHY 4:5–7

5 But watch thou in all things, endure afflictions, do the work of an evangelist, make full proof of thy ministry.

6 For I am now ready to be offered, and the time of my departure is at hand.

7 I have fought a good fight, I have finished my course, I have kept the faith.

Regardless of what obstacles the devil may place in front of you, determine to fight the fight of faith and finish your course. Make that determination right now. Settle it *before* the tests and trials come your way.

I've seen some people who are called to ministry think they finished their course when they graduated from RHEMA Bible Training Center. But that was only the beginning. You haven't finished your course with the Lord until you have fulfilled the calling that He has placed upon your life.

Each of us has a different calling. And each calling is important, because it's from God. I can't tell you what you're called to do in life. Only God can tell you His plan for your future. But whatever it is, the important thing is to finish your course.

Romans 11:29 says, *"For the gifts and calling of God are without repentance."* If you don't have that underlined in your Bible, you need to underline it. When you are tempted to doubt your calling, when you are tempted to doubt God's great plan for your life, this verse will serve to remind you that He does not take back His gifts or His call.

There have been many times when I've been discouraged in life and I was tempted to doubt my calling. Then I would go to Romans 11:29 and read it. *The Amplified Bible* says, "For God's gifts and His call are irrevocable. [He never withdraws them when once they are given, and He does not change His mind about those to whom He gives His grace or to whom He sends His call.]" This verse encouraged me and gave me strength. I knew that I was called. And I knew I had to fulfill that calling.

Friend, let me tell you, God hasn't changed His mind about you. He has called you, and that call will remain.

Hey, God, Why Is It Taking So Long?

You are obligated to fulfill that call. Take God's plan for your life seriously. Decide right now, once and for all, that regardless of the cost, you are determined, as Paul was, to answer and fulfill God's call upon your life.

> **2 TIMOTHY 4:7–8 (NIV)**
>
> **7   I have fought the good fight, I have finished the race, I have kept the faith.**
>
> **8   Now there is in store for me the crown of righteousness, which the Lord, the righteous Judge, will award to me on that day—and not only to me, but also to all who have longed for his appearing.**

I want to receive that crown, don't you? I can hardly wait for the time when the Father will say, "Son, it's time! It's time! Go gather My children and bring them home!" Hallelujah! And as I stand before the Master at the Judgment Seat of Christ, I want to hear those words, "Well done, My good and faithful servant. Enter into the joy of the Lord"!

We are going to be "tested by fire" while we are on the earth. But you can pass the test if you are determined to make it through. And when you have passed through the fire, you will shine as pure gold, spotless and without impurities. You will have been tried and found true, faithful and determined to finish your course with joy.

CHAPTER 6

You Can Totally Rely on God

Is there something God placed within your heart that you have kept secret or protected, wondering for years if you would ever be able to accomplish it? The Lord has brought you to this day as He brought Esther to her day—for such a time as this.

Perhaps you have already accomplished something for God. But He has more planned for your life. You are not "washed up" or "over the hill." Regardless of your age or past achievements, your best is yet to come!

With God, each day is different. He never allows Himself to be put in a box. Some days, there are quiet times. On other days, there are hilarious times. And some days are worshipful times. Just be ready to receive from Him whatever He wants to give you and in whatever manner He wants to give it.

A Lesson in Brenda's Story

I want to recount to you a story I heard. There was a young woman named Brenda who was invited to go rock climbing. Although she was afraid of heights, she went with a group of climbers to a tremendous granite cliff. In spite of her fear, she put on her gear, took hold of the rope, and started up the face of the rock.

She soon reached a ledge where she could take a breather, and she paused because she was a little nervous. As she was hanging there, the safety rope shifted and snapped across her face. One of her contact lenses was knocked from her eye.

You may not know how that feels, but I wear contact lenses, so I know! There Brenda was—on a rock ledge with hundreds of feet above her, and hundreds of feet below her—without her contact lens. She began searching the ledge as best she could, but her contact lens was nowhere to be found.

Brenda was far from home, out of her comfort zone to be sure, and her sight was blurred. She was desperate and began to get upset, so she prayed to God that she find her lens. When Brenda finally reached the top of the mountain, a friend examined her eye and then her clothing to see if the lens was there. It was still nowhere to be found.

Brenda became somewhat despondent. As she was waiting for the rest of her group to reach the top of the cliff, she started praying again. She looked across the range of mountains and said to the Lord, "The Word says that the eyes of the Lord run to and fro throughout the whole earth [2 Chron. 16:9]. Lord, You can see all of these mountains. You know every stone and leaf, and You know exactly where my contact lens is. Please help me find it."

Finally, Brenda and her group went down to the bottom of the cliff. At the bottom, a new party of climbers was waiting to go up. Someone in the new group shouted, "Hey! Has anyone lost a contact lens?"

It was amazing enough that someone had actually *found* a contact lens. Those things are tiny! But it was even more amazing *how* this climber found the contact lens. As he was about to climb, he saw an ant slowly moving across the face of the rock. The ant was carrying the contact lens!

Brenda told her father, a cartoonist, about her story. He drew an ant carrying a contact lens, and the caption beneath the cartoon read, "Lord, I don't know why You want me to carry this thing. I can't eat it, and it's awfully heavy. But if this is what You want me to do, I'll carry it for You."

God Qualifies the Called

Like the ant in that illustration, you may not fully understand God's plan for your life. But His reasons, His ways, and His thoughts are always best. He knows exactly why He has called you to do what He has called you to do. Remember, God doesn't call the qualified. *He qualifies the called!* If you will totally rely on the Lord your God, you will accomplish what He has called you to do.

To successfully fulfill our individual calling, we need to lean on the Lord and totally rely on Him.

PSALM 91:1–2 (*Amplified*)

1   He who dwells in the secret place of the Most High shall remain stable and fixed under the shadow of the Almighty [Whose power no foe can withstand].

2   I will say of the Lord, He is my Refuge and my Fortress, my God; on Him I lean and rely, and in Him I [confidently] trust!

We would think that it would be an easy thing to lean on the Lord, but it is often one of the most difficult things to do. Even the children of Israel had a hard time totally relying on God. It's human nature to want to do everything ourselves. But I firmly believe that in the days ahead, it's going to become an absolute necessity to rely on God in every area of our life.

I've always tried to rely on God, but in recent times, I have had to live out exactly what I'm preaching to you right now. My life is usually busy, but sometimes it's *really* busy! I remember a time when it felt like I was going from one emergency to another.

When Plans Don't Pan Out . . .

We were building dorms at the ranch our church uses for retreats and summer camps. We didn't have adequate housing for campers, so I knew this renovation needed to be done and a deadline had been set for the project.

I had it all planned out. Isn't it wonderful how we plan things out? We think, *Okay, God, I can handle this one myself. You just give me the strength, and I'll take care of everything else.*

Sometimes our plans just don't work! Through those times, God wants to teach us to totally rely on Him. But I hadn't learned to do that yet, so I was busy following everything I had planned out. The construction began in January, and completion was due in June. Immediately after the dorms were finished, I was going to start renovating the Prayer and Healing Center on the RHEMA campus.

We have a gentleman in charge of campus maintenance who was the key player in our remodeling. He completed the dorms just in time for the camps we had scheduled. So I was thinking, *Yes, God, You're right on time! Thank You.*

That left me with the Prayer and Healing Center project that had to be completed by September. I figured June to September gave us plenty of time. But the week we were supposed to start planning the project, one thing after another started happening. Soon, everything began to spiral out of my control, and I needed to rely on God in a hurry!

In the midst of all that was going on, I felt impressed to go to Texas to visit my father. In the natural, I wanted to stay in Tulsa and make sure the renovation got back on course. After all, I had deadlines to meet! But I knew the Holy Spirit was leading me to go, so I obeyed.

Soon after I returned from a weeklong visit with my father, Rev. V.E. Tipton, he went home to be with the Lord. I'm so thankful that I listened to the Lord and was able to spend that time with my dad.

Too many times, we ignore the voice of God. We continue with our agenda instead of obeying God's agenda. It's often hard for us to ignore our deadlines! We have so much on our plate at all times that it's hard for us to give up our to-do list. But it's so important that we totally rely on God. To totally rely on God, we have to trust Him enough to follow His leading even when it doesn't make sense according to our plans. Life tends to work out better when it's out of our control and under God's control.

We had a glorious memorial service for my dad. And even though he was almost 90, I still wasn't ready for my dad to go home. It was like cutting that earthly umbilical cord, and it hurt.

While I was in Dallas for the memorial service, I needed to buy some furnishings for the soon-to-be renovated Prayer and Healing Center. I sure didn't feel like shopping when my dad had just passed away. I was in such a daze that I didn't remember what I bought. I *had to* totally rely on God just to get through the day.

But when I got back to Tulsa and began to unload my purchases, I realized that everything fit perfectly. That project was a spiritual witness to me that I don't have to do things in my own strength or according to my own plans. If I lean on the everlasting arms of God, He will lead me through each situation that comes my way. It is so important to lean on the Lord—to trust in and to rely on Him.

Remember the One From Whom All Blessings Flow

As we rely on God, we will begin to see Him work in every area of our life. God is good, and what He does is good

(Ps. 119:68). In the midst of our experiencing the good life, we must remember the One who made it all possible.

The Lord has blessed each and every one of us. We've been taught the Word of God; we've learned how to use our faith and to exercise our rights and privileges in Christ. But so many times when we receive blessings, we fail to remember the Blesser! We fail to look to our Lord and to thank Him for what He has done for us.

It's time we get back to our first love (*see* Rev. 2:4–5). We must return to the place where we say, "God, whatever Your will is for my life is what I want to do. Not my will, but Yours be done. I'm going to totally rely on You to bring it to pass."

Let's look at one of the greatest biblical examples of trusting God. One of my favorite stories about Abraham—a man who, even though richly blessed by God, still served Him faithfully—is found in Genesis chapter 12.

GENESIS 12:1–4

1 Now the Lord had said unto Abram, Get thee out of thy country, and from thy kindred, and from thy father's house, unto a land that I will shew thee:

2 And I will make of thee a great nation, and I will bless thee, and make thy name great; and thou shalt be a blessing:

3 And I will bless them that bless thee, and curse him that curseth thee: and in thee shall all families of the earth be blessed.

4 So Abram departed, as the Lord had spoken unto him; and Lot went with him: and Abram was seventy and five years old when he departed out of Haran.

Imagine being 75 years old and having God tell you to leave your country, the land in which you've lived for so many years. Not only would that be a traumatic experience, but imagine if the Lord told you to move, but wouldn't tell you where to go! I guarantee you that most of us would not have been as obedient as Abraham.

I don't think we would have quickly obeyed God, but Abraham had learned to totally rely on the Lord. He left his family and all that was his in the land of Haran. I'm sure it was quite a job to pack everything that belonged to him and his wife, but Abraham obeyed God.

Abraham didn't ask, "God, what are Your plans? Before I decide whether or not I want to leave, can You tell me Your 10-year plan? What about Your 5-year plan?" But

Abraham said, "Okay, I'll go. I'll start out in faith and in obedience to you." As Abraham went on his way, God began to lead him in the way he should go.

Too many times, we try to out-plan God. God never gives me a 10-year plan. He doesn't often give me a 5-year plan. I'm doing good to get a 1-year plan! Do you realize that sometimes we have to start out in a certain direction before God will lead us?

'Crazy' Enough to Obey God!

I have already shared about the time in our life when the Lord led us to Oklahoma to work for my father-in-law. We had been associate pastors at my dad's church in Texas, where Ken had pulpit duties, preaching every week. Suddenly, he was Crusade Director for Kenneth Hagin Ministries. That position entailed scheduling meetings for his father, setting up book tables, selling books, setting up chairs in auditoriums, setting up sound systems, doing the announcements, and even being the worship leader sometimes.

It looked like a step backwards! It surely didn't look like the plan God had for our lives. It didn't make sense to us, and it certainly didn't make sense to our friends. They thought we were *crazy*!

But there came a time when God answered my prayers and spoke clearly to us that this was indeed His plan for our life. Then I knew that I knew that I knew that we were supposed to make the move. And thank goodness that I did have that confidence, because a discouraging time came pretty quickly. It wasn't two months later that my husband had the itch to preach and was wondering if he had heard from God after all in making the move to Oklahoma. During that time, I could stand up beside him and say, "Yes, Honey, you obeyed God!"

There are times when wives need to speak up. And there are other times we need to keep our mouth shut. The Spirit of God on the inside lets us know when to speak and what to say. But regardless of what God tells us to do, we have to be "crazy" enough to obey!

Abraham's Faith Is Tested

So Abraham started out in obedience to God. He took the first step, and the Lord began to lead him. Did Abraham have tests along the way? Most assuredly, yes! Even when we determine to totally rely on God, we will still have tests along the way. The first thing Abraham encountered was a famine in the land.

Here Abraham had left his homeland and followed God's leading to a new land. When he arrived, there was a famine! Can you imagine how you would feel in that situation? I can imagine saying, "Um, God, this is the land *You* led me to. Did You know there was a famine here?"

Abraham did just what we might have done. He became afraid and began to question if he had done the right thing. Instead of relying on God, he started relying on his own ability.

GENESIS 12:10–20

10 And there was a famine in the land: and Abram went down into Egypt to sojourn there; for the famine was grievous in the land.

11 And it came to pass, when he was come near to enter into Egypt, that he said unto Sarai his wife, Behold now, I know that thou art a fair woman to look upon:

12 Therefore it shall come to pass, when the Egyptians shall see thee, that they shall say, This is his wife: and they will kill me, but they will save thee alive.

13 Say, I pray thee, thou art my sister: that it may be well with me for thy sake; and my soul shall live because of thee.

14 And it came to pass, that, when Abram was come into Egypt, the Egyptians beheld the woman that she was very fair.

15 The princes also of Pharaoh saw her, and commended her before Pharaoh: and the woman was taken into Pharaoh's house.

16 And he entreated Abram well for her sake: and he had sheep, and oxen, and he asses, and menservants, and maidservants, and she asses, and camels.

17 And the Lord plagued Pharaoh and his house with great plagues because of Sarai Abram's wife.

18 And Pharaoh called Abram, and said, What is this that thou hast done unto me? why didst thou not tell me that she was thy wife?

19 Why saidst thou, She is my sister? so I might have taken her to me to wife: now therefore behold thy wife, take her, and go thy way.

20 And Pharaoh commanded his men concerning him: and they sent him away, and his wife, and all that he had.

Abraham's faith was shaken to the point that he went down to Egypt and acted as if he didn't even know God. He even jeopardized his seed by giving his wife to Pharaoh. I mean, he messed up big! But we serve a forgiving God—the God of second chances. The Lord graciously gave Abraham a second chance.

After the famine, another trial came along—this time in the form of family! Abraham began to have trouble with his nephew, Lot. Abraham's servants were fighting with Lot's servants. There wasn't enough land for all their cattle, so they started fighting over territory.

GENESIS 13:1–11

1 And Abram went up out of Egypt, he, and his wife, and all that he had, and Lot with him, into the south.

2 And Abram was very rich in cattle, in silver, and in gold.

3 And he went on his journeys from the south even to Bethel, unto the place where his tent had been at the beginning, between Bethel and Hai;

4   Unto the place of the altar, which he had made there at the first: and there Abram called on the name of the Lord.

5   And Lot also, which went with Abram, had flocks, and herds, and tents.

6   And the land was not able to bear them, that they might dwell together: for their substance was great, so that they could not dwell together.

7   And there was a strife between the herdmen of Abram's cattle and the herdmen of Lot's cattle: and the Canaanite and the Perizzite dwelled then in the land.

8   And Abram said unto Lot, Let there be no strife, I pray thee, between me and thee, and between my herdmen and thy herdmen; for we be brethren.

9   Is not the whole land before thee? separate thyself, I pray thee, from me: if thou wilt take the left hand, then I will go to the right; or if thou depart to the right hand, then I will go to the left.

10 And Lot lifted up his eyes, and beheld all the plain of Jordan, that it was well watered

every where, before the Lord destroyed Sodom and Gomorrah, even as the garden of the Lord, like the land of Egypt, as thou comest unto Zoar.

11 Then Lot chose him all the plain of Jordan; and Lot journeyed east: and they separated themselves the one from the other.

Abraham realized that he and Lot needed to separate. So he said, "There's not enough land here for both of us. You pick the land that you want, and I'll take the other land." Of course, Lot chose what he thought was the best land. But God knows what is best, and He was looking out for His servant Abraham.

God Is Our Refuge and Defense

You may have been wronged by a friend or relative. You may have been mistreated or abused. But God is still looking out for you. He's going to give you the choice land, so to speak. He has reserved the best for you if you will keep relying on Him.

Have people done things to me that were wrong? Most assuredly, yes! Have people talked badly about me? Yes, they have. Have they said mean things? Yes. Have people tried to hurt me? Yes. What did I want to do in return?

Sometimes I wanted to tell them off! Sometimes I just wanted to cry because my feelings were so hurt.

But I've always chosen the love walk. The love walk causes a person to forgive and forget and not fight back. You see, God is my Defense. Remember what Psalm 91 says: *"He that dwelleth in the secret place of the most High shall abide under the shadow of the Almighty. I will say of the Lord, He is my refuge and my fortress: my God; in him will I trust"* (vv. 1,2). I know if I will keep my eyes on God, He will bring me through to victory every time.

And that's what Abraham did. He trusted in God, knowing God was His Refuge and Fortress. God looked after Abraham because Abraham was following after God.

GENESIS 13:14–16

14 And the Lord said unto Abram, after that Lot was separated from him, Lift up now thine eyes, and look from the place where thou art northward, and southward, and eastward, and westward:

15 For all the land which thou seest, to thee will I give it, and to thy seed for ever.

16 And I will make thy seed as the dust of the earth: so that if a man can number the dust of

**the earth, then shall thy seed also be num-
bered.**

God reassured Abraham that what He had promised,
He would perform. Even still, Abraham grew impatient.
He was getting up in years and no seed had yet been pro-
duced. So he began to question God (Gen. 15:2,8; 17:17).

Sometimes God does not mind us asking Him questions. When Abraham was confused concerning God's
promise, he asked Him about it. Abraham was a friend of
God who loved Him and served Him faithfully, and God
reassuringly answered his question.

GENESIS 15:4–5 (*Amplified*)

**4   And behold, the word of the Lord came to
him, saying, This man shall not be your heir,
but he who shall come from your own body
shall be your heir.**

**5   And He brought him outside [his tent into
the starlight] and said, Look now toward the
heavens and count the stars—if you are able to
number them. Then He said to him, So shall
your descendants be.**

God reassured Abraham again, saying, "Yes, I'm going to perform what I said I would perform if you will simply rely on Me!"

A Meddling Wife Causes Trouble

When the promised seed didn't come when Sarah expected it to come, she decided to help her husband out. Sarah decided to give Abraham her maidservant, so *she* could bear Abraham a child.

GENESIS 16:3–6

3   And Sarai Abram's wife took Hagar her maid the Egyptian, after Abram had dwelt ten years in the land of Canaan, and gave her to her husband Abram to be his wife.

4   And he went in unto Hagar, and she conceived: and when she saw that she had conceived, her mistress was despised in her eyes.

5   And Sarai said unto Abram, My wrong be upon thee: I have given my maid into thy bosom; and when she saw that she had conceived, I was despised in her eyes: the Lord judge between me and thee.

6   But Abram said unto Sarai, Behold, thy maid is in thine hand; do to her as it pleaseth

**thee. And when Sarai dealt hardly with her,
she fled from her face.**

Sarah decided she would help the Holy Ghost! Sometimes wives try to take the place of the Holy Spirit, so to speak, in the lives of their husbands. But God's *timing* is as important as God's *plan*. Sometimes when our plan comes to pass, we realize that what we thought we wanted wasn't what we wanted at all! We can't get ahead of God and expect everything to work out.

Abraham listened to his wife and produced a child, Ishmael, with Hagar as a result. Hagar and Ishmael made life difficult for Sarah, so Sarah got upset and tried to put the blame on Abraham. Abraham told Sarah that the situation was her fault, so she needed to deal with it herself. Sarah dealt so sharply with Hagar that Hagar fled to the wilderness.

Finally, the time came for the promised seed, Isaac, to be born. The Lord came to Abraham and said, "This time next year, a son will be born." Then God changed Abram's name to Abraham, meaning "father of many nations." God also changed Sarai's name to Sarah.

After all Abraham had been through from the time he was 75 and first commanded to leave his country, you would think he would rejoice that his son's birth was so close at hand. Yet how did Abraham respond?

Abraham started laughing! He thought he was too old to bear a child. Genesis 17:17 says, *"Then Abraham fell upon his face, and laughed, and said in his heart, Shall a child be born unto him that is an hundred years old? and shall Sarah, that is ninety years old, bear?"* In verse 18, Abraham starts to bargain with God, saying, "Oh, that Ishmael might live before You!" In other words, Abraham was saying, "Just let the blessing come through Ishmael."

God responded by saying that He would bless Ishmael and multiply his seed, but that the covenant would be with Isaac, not Ishmael. When Sarah heard the Lord say that she would bear a son, she started laughing too!

Sarah probably thought, *Abraham's too old to produce a child, and I'm certainly too old to deliver one!* But when it's the plan and will of God, it shall be done even as the Lord said! And what did He say? *"Is any thing too hard for the Lord? At the time appointed I will return unto thee, according to the time of life, and Sarah shall have a son"* (Gen. 18:14).

Is anything too hard for the Lord? No, nothing is too hard for Him. As long as we learn to trust Him and rely upon Him, it shall be done for us exactly as He has promised.

Trust in the Lord With All Your Heart

Are you ready to say, "Not my timing, Lord, but Yours. Not what I want to do, Lord, but what You want me to do"? You must put your trust in Him, knowing that He's going to take care of you.

PROVERBS 3:5–6

5   Trust in the Lord with all thine heart; and lean not unto thine own understanding.

6   In all thy ways acknowledge him, and he shall direct thy paths.

God is calling on you to trust Him. You may not understand why you have gone through the things you have been through. But the Lord is saying to you, "Trust Me." You may not understand why you're living in the town you're in. But the Lord says, "Trust Me." You may not understand why some of the desires of your heart have not yet come to pass. You may be filled with so many "whys" that you've nearly lost your confidence in God. The Lord is saying to you at this very moment, "Trust Me."

Many times I've wondered, *Why, God? Why did such-and-such happen the way it happened?* Believe it or not, there have been times I wanted to run away from God. But I knew the most important thing I could do in those heartbreaking times was to run as fast as I could *to* God. I knew that trusting Him was my only hope!

What are you facing today? What are some things in your life that are weighing you down? What answers have you been searching for? Sometimes God isn't as quick to answer you as you would like Him to be. His plans often don't unfold as soon as you would have them unfold. Are you willing to wait for the Lord? Are you willing to depend entirely upon Him?

You may be trying to figure out, *How can I make my life work?* You can't make it work! Only God can. But you need to trust in Him. If you will trust Him and not worry and not try to figure everything out, the weight will be lifted. If you will learn the secret of totally trusting in the Lord, He will lead you on a path you never thought possible. The answers will come, and God's plan for your life will unfold in a beautiful and glorious way.

If what I'm saying is ministering to you, witnessing with your spirit, then I believe the following inspired utterance can speak to your heart as well.

*The plan that I have for your life is far greater than
   you could imagine.*

*And though it looks like you have come to a place of
   standing still,*

Hey, God, Why Is It Taking So Long?

Know that I am preparing the way.

Yes, there have been a few detours.

There have been a few rough places that I'm having to smooth out.

But it shall all work out!

Yes, the plan is a little behind, but it's about to accelerate.

It's about to accelerate!

You must learn, because, you see, the reason it's behind

Is, you have not learned the fact of trusting in Me.

I know you tried to figure it out in your head.

You've even lost sleep. You've even experienced physical problems. . . .

The Lord is saying, "Trust in Me. Rely on Me! Rest in Me!

Yes, yes, yes. Rest in Me. Rest in Me. Rest in Me."

Because when there is no rest, there is confusion,

And I can't speak to you . . .

[Because] you can't listen when there's so much confusion in your spirit.

So the Lord is saying, "Rest! Rest. Rest. Rest."

Don't try to figure it out.

For the way you have it figured out is not the way at all, but it shall happen.

That which you have been formulating for many years—it will not be that way.

You're going to be surprised! You're going to be absolutely amazed!

Absolutely shocked! And you're going to say, "God, I can't believe it!

I can't believe it's so easy! It's so easy! Why did I not see it before?"

So take that first step, and as you take that step,

The way will become plainer and plainer and plainer.

And where My voice has been faint, it shall be stronger and stronger and stronger.

And you shall come to a place where there shall be no questions.

Not, "Is this really the direction I was supposed to go?"

No, no! You'll know without a shadow of a doubt.

And you will go in boldness. . . .

For you shall become as a new person. A new person!

And that boldness shall come forth as never before.

And where there has been such trembling, such fear . . .

Hey, God, Why Is It Taking So Long?

[And you've said,] *"God, I don't know how to do this.
I'm so afraid!*

Please let me do something else."

Where there has been all those thoughts of fright,

Out of your mouth shall come a boldness. . . .

And that which I knew from your conception,

that plan shall be consummated.

And no devil in hell shall stop it.

*For you shall take your authority. You shall take your
place.*

You shall take your authority over the wiles of the enemy.

And you shall boldly go forth. . . .

*So I say to you, "Trust in Me. Rely on Me. Let Me do a
new thing in your heart.*

That heart has been so hard. That heart has been so hurt.

*That heart that said, "God, I've been hurt too much! I
can't, I can't, I can't.*

I'm afraid of being hurt."

*The Lord is saying, "I will heal your hurt. I will do a
new thing in your heart.*

Yes, I will heal your memories. I will heal those scars—

Those scars that have been buried so deeply.

Some scars that no one knows about, but they are eating at you . . .

Until you've been so consumed with it that every time you would step out to do what God has called you to do, that thing would just knife you. . . .

God is saying, "I am healing that. I am healing that scar."

The Lord is saying, "You are forgiven! You are forgiven!

So come to Me, for I've placed in you a new heart and a new song.

And you'll go forth. Yes, you'll go forth in My power

And in My might and boldly declare the works of the Lord.

Receive Your Healing

Let the Lord do a work in you. If you need physical healing, He wants to heal your body. If you need emotional healing, He wants to heal your heart. It's okay to yield to Him. Pour out your heart to Him. Let the pain go. Let the past go. Let those hurts and scars and memories all go. Let the Lord do a work in you.

God is not in a hurry. He has all the time in the world for you. Don't believe the lie that it is too late for you. You are not late or running behind. You are right where God wants you, and this is your time.

In order for you to accomplish what God wants you to do, you have to be made whole. You have to be healed inside and out. And God wants to do that. Don't worry about what your spouse might think or what your family or friends might think. Your restoration is too important. God has not forgotten you. He wants to heal you and set you free so that you can be the person He has destined you to be!

Maybe you have become so depressed that you have thought of ending your life. Maybe you think it would be better for your family if you just ended it all. If you've had those thoughts, the Lord wants to deliver you. He sees your situation and what you've been through. Your life is precious to Him! He wants to heal you and turn your situation around so that you can live the long, abundant life on this earth that He has promised you.

As you trust in the Lord and totally rely upon Him, He is going to see you through every step of the way! He will see you through the recovery process, no matter how long it takes to be healed. And He will see you through and cause you to be strong and to minister God's healing power to those around you. Are you ready to trust Him?

CHAPTER 7

Casting Your Cares

One way to speed the recovery process and enter into the total well-being God has for us is to learn how to cast our cares upon the Lord.

Several years ago, when our kids were nearing the age when they would leave home, my husband and I decided that we had better learn to do some activities together. My husband had his hobbies, and I had mine, and every Friday night was family night. The nest was almost empty, and soon the kids would be away at college or married. We decided to develop some interests that we could enjoy together.

I knew if it was going to be something that we did together, it was going to have to somehow involve sports, because there are only about two things that my husband enjoys doing: preaching and playing sports.

Hey, God, Why Is It Taking So Long?

That kind of put me in a dilemma, because my worst talent is sports. If someone throws a ball at me, I'm going to close my eyes when I try to catch it! And that just doesn't work! So I thought, *What on earth are we going to do together? It has to involve sports, and I'm very un-athletic. I don't even like to sweat! And I sure don't like to get my hair or makeup messed up!*

I knew my husband was very good at sports and that, in most cases, I wouldn't have a crying chance of keeping up with him even if I *tried* to learn. So I thought of the two sports that he himself didn't excel in, and those were going to be the two I tried to learn: golf and fishing.

I figured golfing would be okay, because the object of the game involves the ball moving *away* from me. Because the ball doesn't come toward me, I wouldn't have to try to catch it with my eyes closed! Besides that, I had played miniature golf all my life, and thought, *Golf is golf.*

Golf was my husband's worst sport at the time we were trying to come up with a joint hobby, but he has gotten better at it since then. The only other activity I thought that he hadn't done much of was fishing.

So I said, "I will go fishing with you on two conditions: When we use live bait, you bait my hook for me. And if I ever catch a fish, you take it off the hook for me." He was agreeable to that, so we started learning how to fish.

140

We started by first learning to catch small fish that we liked to eat.

We eventually decided that if we wanted to catch bigger fish, we needed a boat to be able to cast in the water. We found a bass boat that was just what we needed, and we started to learn how to fish for bass. We first caught some sand bass by trolling in the water. That was easy to do. However, we decided we needed to catch large-mouth bass. This required casting our lines in the water.

We figured the bass boat qualified us to catch some bass! So we started casting out our lines. I'm telling you, our casting was wild! It was so wild that we were hooking each other's hair! Our casting was not only wild— it was dangerous!

It didn't take us long to realize that we needed to learn how to cast. And it takes casting in order to do some catching! If you want to catch the big prize, you first have to learn how to cast.

I want to talk a little bit about casting. We all need to learn how to cast. But what are we casting? First Peter 5:7 says, *"Casting all your care upon him; for he careth for you."* Psalms 55:22 says, *"Cast thy burden upon the Lord, and he shall sustain thee: he shall never suffer the righteous to be moved."*

Hey, God, Why Is It Taking So Long?

These two verses tell us that we are to cast our cares and our burdens upon the Lord. I prefer to read these verses in *The Amplified Bible*, because as a woman, I want more details! *The Amplified Bible* spells out everything that we are to cast upon the Lord.

1 PETER 5:7 (*Amplified*)

7 Casting the whole of your care [all your anxieties, all your worries, all your concerns, once and for all] on Him, for He cares for you affectionately and cares about you watchfully.

PSALM 55:22 (*Amplified*)

22 Cast your burden on the Lord [releasing the weight of it] and He will sustain you; He will never allow the [consistently] righteous to be moved (made to slip, fall, or fail).

When we cast our burdens on the Lord, He will sustain us. He will never allow us to fail or slip or fall. That means we need to learn to cast our cares upon the Lord!

Learning to cast takes time. It takes practice. And you may not do it perfectly the first few times you do it. It's kind of like when you first cast a fishing line—the first time you try to cast your cares, it may feel like you are catching the hook in your hair!

Start Small and Go From There

Just keep practicing casting your cares upon the Lord. Take it one step at a time. When we started fishing, the first thing we learned to do was just to put our line in the water. We weren't even trying to catch anything. Then we started trying to catch little fish. They were easier to catch than the big ones.

It may be that as you're casting your cares on the Lord, you will find the smaller cares are easier to cast. If you have spent your time worrying about everything and being anxious about everything in life, start with the little things. Start by casting the little cares of life on the Lord. Then as you cast those little things, move on to the bigger things. Just start casting!

We will never be able to pray effectively until we learn to cast our cares upon the Lord. Do you want to know why? Until you cast your cares upon the Lord, every time you begin to pray, those cares will come to your mind. They will begin to consume your thoughts until you either stop praying and start worrying or you start praying about all of your concerns.

You could be on your knees, praying for souls, miracles, healings, and so forth. That lasts about two minutes, and then your prayer changes to, "Oh, God, I need Your help. What am I going to do about such-and-such? And what about this other thing? God, am I going to make it?"

It's time to cast our cares on the Lord, so we can pray effectively for ourselves and for others. It's time to rid ourselves of the worry and anxiety that weighs us down.

1 CORINTHIANS 7:32 (*Amplified*)

32 My desire is to have you free from all anxiety and distressing care. . . .

Are you tired of feeling bound by anxiety and worry? Are you distressed by the cares of this life? The Lord desires for us to be free from anxiety and distressing care. The way we become free is by casting our cares on the Lord.

Worrying Won't Help

Imagine your phone rings early tomorrow morning, you answer it, and you hear a voice say, "Good morning! This is the Lord. Today I will be handling all of your problems. Please remember that I do not need your help in doing so. If the devil happens to deliver a situation to you that you cannot handle, do not attempt to resolve it.

"Kindly put it in the SFJTD (Something For Jesus To Do) box. It will be addressed in My time, not yours. Once the matter is placed into the box, do not hold onto it or

144

attempt to remove it. Holding on or removal will delay the resolution of your problem.

"If it's a situation that you think you're capable of handling, please consult Me in prayer to be sure that it is the proper resolution. Because I do not sleep, nor do I slumber. There is no need for *you* to lose any sleep. Rest, My child. If you need to contact Me, I am only a prayer away."

The author of that inspirational letter is unknown; maybe you've read it somewhere before. But I'm sure that a phone call like that would startle you, right? It would certainly get you thinking!

But we receive that message from God on a daily basis—through His Word! He is daily saying, "Don't worry! Don't fret! Don't be anxious about anything. Don't lose any sleep over anything! Cast the care on Me."

LUKE 12:25–26 (*Amplified*)

25 And which of you by being overly anxious and troubled with cares can add a cubit to his stature or a moment [unit] of time to his age [the length of his life]?

26 If then you are not able to do such a little thing as that, why are you anxious and troubled with cares about the rest?

Hey, God, Why Is It Taking So Long?

Since worrying won't add an inch to our height, or a minute to our life, why are we so busy worrying? It doesn't do anything to help us!

There have been times in my own life when I worried about what to say in a particular situation. I asked God for wisdom according to James 1:5, which says, *"If any of you lack wisdom, let him ask of God, that giveth to all men liberally, and upbraideth not; and it shall be given him."* I needed to know just what I should say and how to say it. In response, the Lord brought Luke 12:11 and 12 to my mind.

LUKE 12:11–12 (*Amplified*)

11 And when they bring you before the synagogues and the magistrates and the authorities, do not be anxious [beforehand] how you shall reply in defense or what you are to say.

12 For the Holy Spirit will teach you in that very hour and moment what [you] ought to say.

If we'll not be anxious but rely on the Holy Spirit, He will teach us what to say in all circumstances. He'll teach us what to say when we go before a banker. He'll teach us what to say whenever we stand before our supervisor on the job. He'll teach us what to say whenever we're reviewing a contract. There is no need to worry or have anxiety about

146

what we should say in any conversation. Now we can cast that care upon the Lord.

Maybe you never get nervous or anxious about what to say. But there might be other situations that cause you to panic or to worry. Regardless of the particular circumstances that affect you, you can begin to go through life without having anxiety about *anything*. How can I say that? God's Word says so!

PHILIPPIANS 4:6–7 (*Amplified*)

6   Do not fret or have any anxiety about anything, but in every circumstance and in everything, by prayer and petition (definite requests), with thanksgiving, continue to make your wants known to God.

7   And God's peace [shall be yours, that tranquil state of a soul assured of its salvation through Christ, and so fearing nothing from God and being content with its earthly lot of whatever sort that is, that peace] which transcends all understanding shall garrison and mount guard over your hearts and minds in Christ Jesus.

When we refuse to fret or have anxiety about anything, life is more enjoyable. When we choose to make our requests known to God in prayer with thanksgiving, God's peace is ours. We can live life in a tranquil state of mind.

Playing by God's Rules

Casting is not always easy, but it's time to start practicing. Of course, the moment we start casting our cares on the Lord, the devil is going to show up the strongest. Notice that right after Peter said, "Cast your cares upon the Lord" in First Peter 5:7, the very next verse warns us to be on guard against the devil.

1 PETER 5:8

8 Be sober, be vigilant; because your adversary the devil, as a roaring lion, walketh about, seeking whom he may devour.

1 PETER 5:8 (*Amplified*)

8 Be well balanced (temperate, sober of mind), be vigilant and cautious at all times; for that enemy of yours, the devil, roams around like a lion roaring [in fierce hunger], seeking someone to seize upon and devour.

When you start casting, you better watch out for the enemy, because he'll show up and try to stop you from casting your cares upon the Lord. He wants you to keep carrying that burden of worry and anxiety. I can see the conversation going a little something like this:

You say, "Lord, I'm casting my care upon You."

The devil brings a situation back to your mind that you used to worry about, saying, "What are you going to do now? Your job is being eliminated; what are you going to do now?"

You continue in faith, "I'm casting my care upon the Lord."

The devil says, "You don't have enough money to pay your bills. What are you going to do now?"

You keep saying, "I've cast the care of that on the Lord. He cares about my finances, so I'm not worried. His Word says that *all* my needs are met according to His riches in glory [Phil. 4:19]!"

The devil tries another tactic, saying, "Your body is racked with pain. What are you going to do?"

You counter again, "I'm casting my care upon the Lord. First Peter 2:24 says that I've been healed by the stripes of Jesus. I'm not worried or anxious about my body any longer. The Lord is taking care of that for me."

Do you get it? We're in the game of life, but we don't have to play by the devil's rules. We play by *God's* rules. And God's rules say *to cast our cares upon the Lord.*

Don't Allow the Devil to Distract You

Several years ago, I began to be concerned about some things. I tried not to worry about them, but every time I'd think about a particular situation, I started worrying about it. I knew I was supposed to cast my care upon the Lord, and I would try to do just that.

The devil would bring it back again and again. I would cast the care, and the devil would bring it back—on and on this went until the Lord revealed something to me. He said, "These worried thoughts are mere distractions to keep you from doing what I have called you to do." *Mere distractions!* I decided then and there to stop letting the devil distract me from my calling.

You have a destiny to fulfill. Don't allow the devil to distract you with worry, fear, and anxiety. Not only will those emotions harm you mentally and spiritually, they will eventually start to harm you physically.

Worry is a sin, and worry will make you sick—physically sick. Satan will purposely create things for you to worry about. He wants you distracted and distressed and sick.

So right now, purpose in your heart that you will not worry. How do you keep from worrying? Get rid of whatever things you are tempted to worry about. How do you get rid of them? By casting them upon the Lord!

It may help you to physically stand up where you are and go through the actual motions of casting a fishing line. Imagine your hook is hooked onto all the cares you have been carrying. Then lean back and cast that line of cares out beyond you—casting them upon the Lord because He cares for you!

You may have financial cares right now. Cast them away. You may have family problems. Cast them upon the Lord. Of course, He expects us to do our part in the natural. But when you have done everything you can do, cast the rest upon the Lord. He will take care of it!

Once we have cast our concerns upon the Lord, we can start praying out *His* concerns and *His* plans. As you cast your cares on the Lord, say, "Once and for all, I'm casting these cares upon the Lord, never to receive them back in my thought life."

The following is a prophetic utterance I received from the Lord in a meeting in which I ministered.

As you cast your care upon the Lord, you shall rise.

You shall rise to a level as you've never seen before.

Hey, God, Why Is It Taking So Long?

For you see, My voice has been so dim.

But as you walk with Me without distractions,

That voice shall speak stronger and stronger . . .

And I will move you to a level you've not seen before. . . .

And as you seek My face, yes, as you seek My face

And pray My will and My desires—

Not your will, not your desires—

But [you] come with an open heart and say,

"God, what would You have me pray tonight?"

As you do that, revelation after revelation [will flow]. . . .

But you must each take your place,

Willing to commit,

Willing to set aside time to commune with Me,

Willing to give of your time.

And now is the time to shed all those weights.

To shed all those weights that can so easily beset you!

Now is the time to simplify your life

And get back to making Me the center of your life.

And as you make Me the center of your life,

As you make Me the center of your home, things will change.

Things will change around you.

And where there has been trouble, there shall be peace.

And where there has been frustration, there shall be tranquility.

So make Me the center. Make Me the center!

And simplify, simplify, simplify. . . .

As we seek the Lord to develop this kind of relationship with our Heavenly Father, He is going to give us boldness where we need boldness. He's going to give us strength where we need strength. He's going to give us wisdom where we need wisdom. And He's going to give us peace where we need peace.

He will carry us through all the trials that may come our way. He will carry us through all the hard places—right through them! And we will come out rejoicing on the other side.

I want to do God's will. How about you? Are you yearning for more? Are you wanting to go higher? Are you ready to go further in His Presence? Let's begin by casting our cares upon the Lord.

If it takes practice, *practice!* Don't worry about it; sleep soundly. And if you awaken with worry, say it again, "I'm casting my cares on the Lord." Peace, tranquility, wholeness, wellness—these and more shall be yours as you learn to trust and rest in the Lord!

CHAPTER 8

Peace in Troubled Times

Peace, tranquility, wholeness, wellness—sound too good to be true? In the world in which we live, there seems to be trouble on every side. Read the newspapers and you will find wars, earthquakes, floods, crime, and every type of calamity you can imagine. It seems that tragedy is all we ever hear about in the news.

We also live in a world where we have more conveniences, more technology, and more luxuries than ever before. Some kitchens have three microwaves—one for each item in the meal. All three cook food at the same time and—*presto!*— dinner is served.

You would think with all these technological advances, we would have more time! But, instead, we find that we have less time. And you would also think there would be peace. But in a world with seemingly every modern convenience, still there is no peace.

Of course, we cannot have peace without knowing Jesus, the Prince of Peace, as our Lord and Savior. Romans 5:1 says, *"Therefore being justified by faith, we have peace with God through our Lord Jesus Christ."* God made provision for us to have peace.

When God first created man, there was peace in the Garden of Eden. Then man sinned, and there was no peace. But, thank God, He loved us so much that He sent His only Son that we might have life and that we might have it more abundantly (John 3:16; 10:10). With that abundant life comes the blessing of peace.

JOHN 14:27

27 Peace I leave with you, my peace I give unto you: not as the world giveth, give I unto you. Let not your heart be troubled, neither let it be afraid.

If you ever wonder how valuable you are, just think of what God did for you. He sent His one and only Son. I don't know about you, but I don't know if I could have done that for mankind. I think I might have just said, "You messed up, so you're going to have to live with it." But, thank God, He did not say that to us. He said, "Yes, you messed up. [We messed up royally!] But I'm going to send My one and only Son to redeem you."

I'm reminded of a story of a little boy who was praying, and at the end of his prayer, he said, "And, God, please take care of Yourself, because if anything happened to You, we'd all be in a mess."

Isn't that the truth? We would all be in a mess if it weren't for God!

As I said, in order to have peace, we must know the One who gives peace. Unfortunately, many people who know Christ as their Savior do not know Him as their Peace-Giver. He's not only our Savior, but He is also our Peace-Giver.

It's sad that more and more people, even Christians, are turning to anti-depressants and other drugs to give them peace. For some people, even for children, these drugs seem to be the answer to all of life's problems. For children in need of peace, the first thing given is a prescription drug. It is sad that even in the Christian world, the use of prescription drugs is so commonplace.

God can get you through the storms of life. God can help you in every situation, and you won't have to alter your body chemistry. In troubled times, God's Word can help you cope with everyday life without the aid of chemicals.

Tranquilizers can give you only temporary peace. But God can give you *permanent* peace! He is the Problem *Solver*. I'm not teaching you something that I haven't practiced in my own life. In fact, I have to practice this on a daily basis.

One passage of Scripture I have to rely upon on a daily basis is Isaiah 26:3 and 4.

ISAIAH 26:3–4

3 Thou wilt keep him in perfect peace, whose mind is stayed on thee: because he trusteth in thee.

4 Trust ye in the Lord for ever: for in the Lord Jehovah is everlasting strength.

ISAIAH 26:3–4 (*Amplified*)

3 You will guard him and keep him in perfect and constant peace whose mind [both its inclination and its character] is stayed on You, because he commits himself to You, leans on You, and hopes confidently in You.

4 So trust in the Lord (commit yourself to Him, lean on Him, hope confidently in Him)

forever; for the Lord God is an everlasting Rock [the Rock of Ages].

Have you committed yourself to the Lord? Do you lean on Him? I lean on Him on a daily basis. Every day when I wake up, I say, "God, I have to make decisions about such-and-such today. But I don't have the answers. You said in Your Word, in James 1:5, that if anyone lacks wisdom, he can ask of You and You will give to him liberally. God, I don't know the answers, but I am leaning on You. You are the reason I can have peace in this situation."

If you'll lean on the Lord, He will give you the strength and wisdom and peace that you need and desire.

Isaiah 26:4 in *The Amplified Bible* says, "So trust in the Lord (commit yourself to Him, lean on Him, hope confidently in Him) forever; for the Lord God is an everlasting Rock [the Rock of Ages]."

We can stand on the Rock. The Rock will never crumble; this Rock won't even shift or shake. The Rock, the Lord Jesus, never shakes! We have a solid foundation when we stand on that Rock.

What is peace? The dictionary defines it this way: *a state of tranquility or quiet; freedom from disquieting or oppressive thoughts or emotions.* The Hebrew word "shalom" carries the meaning of wholeness, harmony, well, happy, friendly, health, something complete and sound, and prosperity.[1] This infers the idea of *soundness of health, physically, mentally, emotionally, and spiritually.*

We know from God's Word that God has provided health for us. But so many times, we take that promise only to mean spiritual or physical health. But God has also promised us emotional and mental health. We can be healed in every area of our life.

The problem is, most of us try to live a peaceful and victorious life without keeping our mind on the Lord Jesus Christ. According to Isaiah 26:3, which says, *"Thou wilt keep him in perfect peace, whose mind is stayed on thee,"* we must keep our mind on Jesus if we want to live in peace.

Many times this is what happens: We have our mind stayed on Christ and life starts to go pretty good for us. At first we shout, "Hallelujah, this is wonderful!" Then because life is going so good, we tend to forget about the Lord. We forget about keeping our mind on Him. And we start having more and more confidence in ourselves.

We can never have confidence in our abilities because in ourselves alone, we are nothing. It is only through Christ that we can accomplish all things—and that is because *He* strengthens us (Phil. 4:13).

So many times when everything is going good, we slack off in our relationship with our Heavenly Father. But if we're going to live a peaceful life, our relationship with God must be continually growing, not diminishing.

I've heard testimonies from people who were in adverse circumstances, and they said, "I'm thankful for the trial because it brought me closer to God." Thank God, they got closer to Him, but we don't need a trial to bring us closer to God. We can stay close to God all the time!

Unfortunately, the natural tendency is to kind of drift away from our relationship with God when everything is going fine. Then, suddenly, when something bad happens, we run to God for help. Yes, He's there for us when we're in trouble, just like an earthly parent would be there to help his child. But it's much better for us if we commune with our Heavenly Father on a regular basis. We can stay close to Him daily, and by doing so, daily live in peace.

In natural parent-child relationships, children often wander away and do their own thing away from their parents. But when they get in trouble, where do they go? They go back to Mom and Dad. When they get in a financial bind, who do they call? They call Mom and Dad. And most natural parents are there to help when their children are in need. But I guarantee most parents would rather have had a relationship with that child all along—not just in the hard times.

Serving God should be a way of life, not just a Sunday morning experience. We can stay close to God on a daily basis, but the choice is ours. In today's world, few people choose to make God the center of their life. It's sad to say, but even Christians rarely choose to keep God first.

With so many sports and activities for kids, children today often go from one game to another to another. They are involved in this, that, and the other thing. For many Christian families, church takes a back seat to other activities. That grieves my heart. We need to get back to the place where our Heavenly Father and His plans are the very center of our life. We need to return to the place where everything we do revolves around Him—that is the place where we will find peace.

Some people downplay the emotional part of the salvation experience. But I'm so thankful for the day I went to the altar to give my life to God. Remembering the experience I had when I accepted Jesus as Savior and made Him Lord of my life has kept me through many storms of life. When I'm tempted to put other things ahead of God or when life seemingly begins to crumble under my feet, remembering the precious relationship I have with Jesus as my Lord and Savior is what gets me through.

Just because we became a Christian doesn't mean that everything in life will be easy. We're going to go through trials. We're going to walk through valleys sometimes. But we don't have to camp in those valleys. Now we can walk *through* them, knowing that our Lord is going to be with us every step of the way.

Jesus Obtained Our Peace

Isaiah 53 tells us that Jesus bore our sickness and our pain. But in the storms of life, I am comforted when I remember what else Isaiah 53 says that Jesus bore for me.

ISAIAH 53:4–5 (*Amplified*)

4 Surely He has borne our griefs (sicknesses, weaknesses, and distresses) and carried our sorrows and pains [of punishment], yet we [ignorantly] considered Him stricken, smitten, and afflicted by God [as if with leprosy].

5 But He was wounded for our transgressions, He was bruised for our guilt and iniquities; the chastisement [needful to obtain] peace and well-being for us was upon Him, and with the stripes [that wounded] Him we are healed and made whole.

Jesus bore my grief and my sorrow. He also bore the chastisement needed to obtain my peace and well-being. I no longer have to bear distress or pain or sorrow, because Jesus bore it all for me on the Cross.

Put God First

Because Jesus gave His all for me, I want to give my all for Him. That requires commitment. But when we commit our way to the Lord, the result is always peace.

Psalm 37:5 says, *"Commit thy way unto the Lord; trust also in him; and he shall bring it to pass."* If most Christians were honest, we would admit that sometimes we commit our way to the Lord, and other times, we don't. But if we're going to live a peaceful life, we must commit all of our ways to Him—all the time. If you haven't been enjoying peace in life, check to see if you have committed all your ways to the Lord. Is there an area that you have been holding back from Him? Is there an area in which you wanted to follow your own way, so you haven't committed that area to the Lord?

The Word promises that all we need in life will be added to us if we will just seek first the Kingdom of God (Matt. 6:33). So if we're not having "all of those things" added to us, we need to check up on what we have been seeking. Are we seeking material possessions? Are we seeking position? Are we seeking fame or fortune? Are we seeking success?

Certainly, we all want to be successful. But how do we become successful? By seeking first the Kingdom of God and by placing Him first in our life. Part of putting God first means surrounding ourselves with the Word of God.

We live in a busy world. We don't have a lot of spare time. If something comes up in your day, and you don't think you have enough time to spend time in prayer or in reading the Word concerning your situation, you can at least try to surround yourself with the Word of God in some form.

I play Christian music in our house literally 24 hours a day. I have my five favorite CDs, loaded with songs about the Word of God, about the Blood, and about the Cross, and the songs play over and over in our house. Whether we're there or not, those songs are playing in our house continually. You see, I want our house filled with the Word of God. When I walk into my house, I want to know the anointing of God has permeated every inch of my home.

When I wake up in the morning, I hear the music; if I wake up in the middle of the night, I instantly hear songs from the Word. Remember, God will give us peace if we'll keep our mind on Him.

165

That's just one example of what I mean by surrounding yourself in an atmosphere charged with the peace and Presence of God. Anointed music with godly lyrics is just one way you can surround yourself with the Word when you may feel like you don't have time to spend an hour reading the Bible.

Another thing I do is play encouraging Christian music whenever I'm in my car. I need that. I have to have it in order to keep my mind in peace.

I meditate on the Lord and His Word constantly. We like to fellowship with our friends, don't we? Well, God is my Best Friend. I can tell Him anything. When I need something in life, I go to God and tell Him about it. He's my Best Friend, and I talk to Him real and plain—just like I would a best friend!

One time I needed an answer to a situation and I said, "God, I feel like I need a sign. I know You've told us to walk by faith, and You know that I do walk by faith. But, Lord, this is how I'm feeling."

I don't hide what I'm feeling from God. He knows anyway! So I am always honest with Him about my feelings. He is concerned about whatever we're concerned about. And He wants us to talk to Him. He said in James 4:2 that we have not because we ask not. He also said that if we will ask for something according to His will, He will give us whatever we ask of Him.

1 JOHN 5:14–15 (*NIV*)

14 This is the confidence we have in approaching God: that if we ask anything according to his will, he hears us.

15 And if we know that he hears us—whatever we ask—we know that we have what we asked of him.

As a parent, I just love giving my child something he or she has asked for. How much more does our Heavenly Father love us and love giving good things to us? Matthew 7:11 says, *"If ye then, being evil* [or natural]*, know how to give good gifts unto your children, how much more shall your Father which is in heaven give good things to them that ask him?"*

God is concerned about your life. He wants to give you good things and to give you His peace. There are several important things we must do in order to receive the peace God has for us. We need to have an intimate relationship with Him; we need to read His Word; we need to pray; and we must guard our thoughts.

Defeating a Defeated Foe

It's important that we allow the Heavenly Father to be our Best Friend. It's also important that we read the Word of God, because if we're going to ask for things "according to His will," we need to know what His will is. And if we're going to keep our mind in peace, we need to keep our mind on the Word. There are many scriptures in the Bible on the subject of peace. Find those scriptures, read them, take them to heart, and think about them throughout the day, and they will give you peace.

It's also important that we pray, spending time talking to God on a regular basis. And if we want to live a truly peaceful life, we must also guard our mind and control our thought life. It's important that *we* do something about our thoughts.

The mind can be a powerful ally or an awesome enemy. God has said that our mind will stay in perfect peace if we will keep our mind (our thoughts) on the Lord.

The enemy is out to get you. According to John 10:10, he is out to steal from you, to kill you, and to destroy you. First Peter 5:8 says, *"Be sober, be vigilant; because your adversary the devil, as a roaring lion, walketh about, seeking whom he may devour."*

Notice this verse doesn't say that Satan *is going* to devour you. It says he *is seeking* for someone he *may* devour. In other words, he is searching for people who will allow him to devour them.

But what does the previous scripture say? First Peter 5:7 says, *"Casting all your care upon him; for he careth for you."* We don't need to cast just part of our care on the Lord. This verse says to cast *all* of it on Him.

Satan specializes in worry. He specializes in fear. He specializes in anxiety, confusion, and doubt. Those are his specialties. And he'll bring those to your mind if you allow him to do so. The devil is not a gentleman like the Holy Spirit. If you crack the door open just a little bit, the devil will kick it wide open. And your mind is the bull's eye of Satan's target. That's why the Bible says we're not to give place to the devil (Eph. 4:27). Don't allow him to dominate your thought life.

If you allow yourself to think negative thoughts, you'll be defeated. If you allow yourself to worry, you'll be defeated. If you allow yourself to be in fear, you'll be defeated.

You cannot think defeat and expect victory. You cannot think sickness and expect health. You cannot think poverty and expect wealth. Whatever you allow yourself to think on *will become* what you expect. And that will be exactly what you receive.

I know we live in a negative society. Take one look at the news. It's not "news" unless it's bad. The good that happens is no longer considered newsworthy. Even in the Christian world, we are quicker to tell the bad things that have happened rather than the good things. For example, you rarely see someone rush up to you at church and say, "Did you hear about Preacher So-and-so? Their marriage is so strong! They are really great examples to the Body of Christ." No, it's just the opposite that most people are so quick to talk about.

Satan constantly bombards our minds with negative thoughts. He's constantly trying to confuse us and keep us from the peace that we can experience with God. And Satan will succeed unless we replace the negative thoughts with positive thoughts from God's Word.

God Gives Peace for Fear

As I said, Satan specializes in fear. I know because it was something he used against me in my life for a long time. I did not like to fly in airplanes. Whenever I had to fly, a spirit of fear would try to grip me. If you've never experienced that kind of fear, believe me, it's a horrible feeling. Well, because of what we do in the ministry, I had to fly a lot.

The fear got so bad that I realized I had to do something about it in order to be able to continue flying. I found some scriptures to stand on so that fear could not dominate my mind. Every time I got on a plane, I read those scriptures. Psalm 121:4–8 was one passage I read.

PSALM 121:4–8

4   Behold, he that keepeth Israel shall neither slumber nor sleep. [I was so thankful that God was not sleeping while I was on the plane.]

5   The Lord is thy keeper: the Lord is thy shade upon thy right hand.

6   The sun shall not smite thee by day, nor the moon by night.

7   The Lord shall preserve thee from all evil: he shall preserve thy soul.

8   The Lord shall preserve thy going out and thy coming in from this time forth, and even for evermore.

As the plane lifted off the runway, I said, "The Lord is going to preserve me as I'm taking off, and He's going to preserve me when I'm touching down."

Hey, God, Why Is It Taking So Long?

That spirit of fear dominated me to the point where I literally trembled whenever there was any kind of turbulence on the plane. Sometimes I gripped my husband's hand so tightly that it turned red and was almost bruised from my grip.

Even though I was claiming the promises of God every time I got on an airplane, it took time for those promises to come to pass in my life—for my mind to believe more firmly on God's Word than upon the negative thoughts and feelings of fear. It was a gradual process during which my faith had to develop.

Eventually, I got to where I could travel by plane, but it had to be a *big* plane. I still wouldn't travel on a private plane, because they were too small, and my faith wasn't there yet.

However, a fellow minister told us that God wanted us to have a plane to protect the anointing on our lives. I knew he was right. In order to meet the demanding ministry schedule of preaching all over the world, visiting more than a dozen RHEMA Bible Training Centers located in different countries, we were going to need a private aircraft. Flight times were shorter, and there were no scheduling problems, flight delays, long layovers, or long flights with no rest. With a private airplane, we could travel farther and faster—and arrive more rested than if we had flown commercial.

I knew all this, but my mind was still whirling because of my battle with fear. I knew that a private plane would be much smaller. I wasn't sure I could handle that. For the few days after we first talked about needing a private plane, I walked around in a daze. I smiled and said "hi" to people, but I wasn't really seeing anyone because my mind was giving me trouble.

All of this mental turmoil over flying in a private plane reached its climax several years ago during the week of Campmeeting. I will never forget the service on the last night of the week. It was a Saturday evening, and my mind was just whirling. I was thinking, *God, I know traveling by private plane is the right thing to do, but I cannot live in this turmoil and fear. I already have to stand on the Word every time I get in a commercial jet, and even when I do, I still have trouble with my mind. If I'm to get into a smaller plane, I need to really get over this completely.*

That night, as Brother Hagin was closing the service, he said, "Let us pray." He didn't know what I was going through; he didn't even know Ken and I had talked about a private plane. But, suddenly, instead of closing the service, he said, "Some of you here are dealing with fear, and

Hey, God, Why Is It Taking So Long?

God wants to deliver you this very night. Everyone who is dealing with fear, stand up."

When I heard him say that, I knew it was my night to be delivered once and for all from the spirit of fear. And yet as I sat there, I thought, *God, You know that I need to stand up. And you know that I really don't mind standing and admitting that I need to be delivered. But the minute I stand up, everyone will see me and say, "What could she have a problem with? Why is she standing up?"*

So there I was with my mind whirling, *Should I, or shouldn't I?* (Those thoughts come to preachers just like they come to others.) Suddenly, I felt a rustling behind me and thought someone behind me was standing up. So I kind of peeked and saw that a well-known minister had stood up.

I thought, *God, if he can stand up, I can stand up too! This is my night! I'm going to be delivered from this terrible fear that has gripped me for so long.* I stood up. Brother Hagin prayed a prayer, and there were no instant manifestations. I just took it by faith that fear would not dog me anymore.

Of course, I needed to test it out—to actually fly and prove that the fear was gone. But I didn't know that I would be tested so soon. Shortly after Campmeeting, I had to travel with my husband, and the only way we were able to make the trip was by a small private plane. To make a long story short, when we were about to take off, the wind was blowing at what seemed to be 90 miles an hour. I saw my husband gulp, and I was sure he was thinking, *What's my wife going to do in this airplane with all of this wind?*

I remember wondering why the first test had to be in such a strong circumstance, but I got up in that plane and had no fear! Hallelujah! And I haven't had any fear since! Glory to God for His peace!

The anointing of the Spirit will break every yoke of bondage in your life. If you have been wrestling and wrestling and wrestling with something in your life, I want to pray this prayer for you.

I believe that yoke of bondage is broken in the Name of Jesus. Yes, that yoke is broken in the Name of Jesus. We stand against those powers of darkness. We stand against those principalities. We bind together to break those forces. Those strongholds must come down. For we speak the Name of Jesus, the Name that is above all names, and at the Name of Jesus, every knee must bow. Every tongue must confess that Jesus Christ is Lord. Every obstacle will be removed. Every stronghold will come down! Yes, those walls are coming down. Those barriers that have held you back, those barriers are coming down.

Hey, God, Why Is It Taking So Long?

You have struggled so long, but now those walls are coming down. In Jesus' mighty Name.

It's time for you to march around your Jericho. Whatever it is that you are fighting against or struggling with, I want you to imagine it as a fortress—a mighty Jericho that stands between you and what you are believing God for. I want you to imagine yourself marching around that Jericho; get up and march right where you are if you have to. March around those walls and envision them crumbling to the ground! Begin to thank God for what He is doing in your situation. Praise Him for what He's done in your life in the past; thank Him for what He is doing now and for what He *will* do. Praise Him *now*, even while the walls may still be standing. Because it will only be a matter of time before your praises are for a promise that *has come to pass*!

Don't lose your joy. Your answer could be just around the corner! Don't give up, because victory is just around the corner. Stand firm and stand strong!

If you have been dealing with fear, in the Name of Jesus, I take authority over that fear. Fear, you must leave in the Name of Jesus. God has not given us a spirit of fear, but a spirit of power, love, and a sound mind (2 Tim. 1:7). That fear must go, in the Name of Jesus.

Keeping Your Mind on Things Above

The Lord will keep us in perfect peace; He will deliver us. We don't have to fear. We don't have to worry. But we must keep our mind on the Lord Jesus Christ as we read in Isaiah 26:3. Philippians chapter 4 tells us exactly how to do that.

PHILIPPIANS 4:4–8

4   Rejoice in the Lord always: and again I say, Rejoice.

5   Let your moderation be known unto all men. The Lord is at hand.

6   Be careful for nothing; but in every thing by prayer and supplication with thanksgiving let your requests be made known unto God.

7   And the peace of God, which passeth all understanding, shall keep your hearts and minds through Christ Jesus.

8   Finally, brethren, whatsoever things are true, whatsoever things are honest, whatsoever things are just, whatsoever things are pure, whatsoever things are lovely, whatsoever things are of good report; if there be any virtue, and if there be any praise, think on these things.

You need to think on the things that will build you up and not tear you down. Think on the things that God has done for you. Focus on the positive.

If you're thinking about the good things of God, you're not going to have time to worry and complain and get down and discouraged. If you're meditating on God's promises, you're going to be filled with a good report. And His report says, "I am healed." His report says, "I am more than a conqueror." His report says, "I am rich and not poor." His report says, "I can do all things through Christ who strengentheth me." His report says, "I have a sound mind." His report says, "I will always triumph." And His report says, "It shall come to pass."

Whatever the Lord has said to you shall come to pass. What God promises in His Word shall come to pass. Whatever you are believing God for, hang on! It shall come to pass.

So stop thinking about what you *don't* have and start thinking about what you *do* have. Stop thinking about what is *wrong* with you and start thinking about what is *right* with you. Stop thinking about how big your *problem* is and start dwelling on how big your *God* is! He is bigger than any problem you may face! He is big enough to meet all your needs and to deliver you from any situation. He is big enough to bring you peace in the midst of any storm!

In life, situations and circumstances are constantly changing. But our God never changes (Mal. 3:6). He is the same yesterday, today, and forever (Heb. 13:8).

When you keep your mind on the Lord, it doesn't matter what the stock market does. Because God said He would supply all of your needs according to His riches in glory (Phil. 4:19). He didn't say He would meet *part* of your needs; He said He would meet *all* of them. So it doesn't matter what the economy does. God still can rain down manna from Heaven. He hasn't lost the recipe! Therefore, the most important thing we can ever do is to put our trust in God.

There's an old song that says, in effect, "I trust in God wherever I may be, upon the mount, or on the lowly sea. Though come what may from day to day, my heav'nly Father watches over me."[2] Friend, God is watching over you. He cares about what you're going through.

If you are struggling and facing difficulties right now, I encourage you find scriptures that talk about your situation. Stand on those scriptures. Take the Word of God like medicine. In other words, read the Word and say it out loud several times a day. Make the scripture personal by putting your name and situation into the verse, and God's medicine will work for you! It will heal your mind and body. It will heal your emotions. It will heal your home. It will bring your children back. And there will be no ill side effects!

I encourage you today to trust in the Lord. As you meditate on Him and His Word amidst the stormy seas and times of trouble, He will give you peace, and His peace that passes understanding will guard your heart and mind in Christ Jesus (Phil. 4:7) and keep you safe on the journey ahead.

---

[1] Lawrence O. Richards, *Expository Dictionary of Bible Words* (Grand Rapids: Zondervan Publishing House, 1991), 479; James Strong, *The New Strong's Exhaustive Concordance of the Bible* (Nashville: Thomas Nelson Publishers, 1984), 116.

[2] W.C. Martin and Charles H. Gabriel, "My Father Watches Over Me" (I Trust in God), © 1910 Charles H. Gabriel, © renewed 1938 (extended) The Rodeheaver Co.

CHAPTER 9

How to Receive and Fulfill God's Plan

Having cast our cares upon the Lord, we will be able to enjoy life more. When our mind is stayed on the Lord, He will keep us in perfect peace. But even then, our body sometimes gets a little tired, and we get a little weary. All we have to do in those times is call upon the Lord.

When I'm tired, I confess that the same Spirit that raised Christ from the dead dwells in me. I claim that the Spirit will quicken my mortal body (Rom. 8:11). I thank the Lord for good sleep each night, and I thank Him that He is redeeming my time. I rest in Him and am strengthened by Him.

Romans 8:11 says, "And if the Spirit of him who raised Jesus from the dead is living in you, he who raised Christ from the dead will also give life to your mortal bodies through his Spirit, who lives in you" (*NIV*). In these last days, with all that we have been called to do, we're going to need a quickening of the mortal body! We're going to need lots of strength in the natural, because we've got a big job to do. We've got a big task. And we can't be saying, "I'm so tired."

Believe me, if you keep saying you're tired, you're going to be tired! I hear young people all the time—people much younger than I am—saying how tired they are. Most of the time, they're not tired; they're bored. But if they start saying they're tired now—and keep saying it—wait until they get to be my age! They won't even be able to get out of bed!

Our world is formed by the words of our mouth (Matt. 12:37; Mark 11:23; Rom. 10:10). With my words, I am creating a long life (Ps. 91:16; Prov. 16:23–24). I am creating a productive life and a life that will be filled with strength and energy from the Lord (Num. 13:30; Josh. 14:10–12). I know that our world is formed by our words, so you won't find me saying, "I'm tired." I don't want that to become reality by the words of my mouth. Instead, I create a new reality by saying, "I am strengthened in the Lord. I have the energy to do what I need to do according to the assignment I have received from Him." If you start confessing "I am strong" instead of "I am tired," you will be surprised at how much better you feel. God will use your mouth to strengthen you.

I have so much energy that people often ask me what kind of vitamins I take. For years, I didn't take any vitamins at all. I just recently started taking vitamins because I realized that at my age, I would have to consume too many calories for the vitamins needed. One source of energy and personal encouragement I use is a regular dose of laughter!

Laughter does something wonderful for you. It offers emotional relief and physical relief. We all need to laugh—some days more than others. Sometimes our friends can cheer us up; other times God will take an ordinary part of life and use it to bring us cheer.

For example, I remember once a friend of mine was having a bad day. She called me at work and asked, "Do you like me?"

I thought, *What planet is she from? Of course I like her!* I said, "Yes, I like you. Why?"

She said, "I'm having problems today. I don't think anyone likes me. I just had to find someone who likes me."

So I started to tell her a funny story I had heard that day in order to cheer her up. We went from one story to another. Soon my friend was laughing uncontrollably.

Hey, God, Why Is It Taking So Long?

And at the end of our conversation, she thanked me for cheering her up, saying, "I needed to laugh today."

We all have bad days in which we need some cheering up too. It's amazing what God will use to minister to us. Sometimes He uses a friend or loved one, and other times He uses a less likely source.

I remember one occasion on which I really needed cheering up. It was the Sunday after my father's memorial service. I had gone to a local church in Texas, because I needed to receive ministry. But I didn't seem to receive what I needed at that time.

I went back to our hotel and took a nap. When I woke up, depression started trying to take hold of me. I recognized that depression and knew I had to do something about it.

I thought, *I need to hear something from the Lord.* So I turned on the television, thinking I would find some Christian programming and be able to receive ministry that way.

I started flipping through the channels. I could not find any Christian channels on that TV. I kept flipping and flipping, thinking, *God! I have to have something! I'm sinking deep and need something to lift my spirits.*

Suddenly, I tuned into "Larry King Live." You may wonder how on earth this show could minister to me. This particular evening, Mr. King had television personality Art Linkletter on his program. I didn't even know Art Linkletter was still around! I remembered watching his shows "People Are Funny" and "Kids Say the Darndest Things." I had always admired Art Linkletter.

That night Art Linkletter was celebrating his ninetieth birthday—and he looked great! Larry King asked him what his secret to success was and how he kept himself so young. Linkletter replied, in effect, "For one thing, I've never quit learning. I'm always looking to learn something. And another thing, I've always kept laughter in my heart. I always laugh."

This might sound crazy, but by the time I got through listening to the program, I was laughing and my spirits were raised too! God can use anything to cheer us up and brighten our day.

Many times we fail to look at the little things in life that could serve as encouragement for us. We think God has to answer our prayers a certain way. But we must learn to receive whatever God gives to encourage and help us.

The Strength of the Lord

Laughter can do our body good. But the most important vitamin I take is the strength of the Lord! I take the "vitamins" of praying in the Spirit and reading God's Word. Those things alone give me energy like nothing the world gives.

If the same Spirit that raised Christ from the dead dwells in you, it will quicken your mortal body and make you strong (Rom. 8:11). When you're tempted to say "I'm tired," say "I'm strong in the Lord" instead.

When you need inspiration, think of Caleb in the Old Testament. Caleb was 85 years old when he possessed the mountain God had promised to him 45 years earlier.

Caleb remained faithful and believed God's Word for 45 years. Talk about a season of waiting! Caleb knew when to believe God and patiently wait, and he knew when the waiting was over and it was time to take possession of what God had promised him.

JOSHUA 14:6–12

6 Then the children of Judah came unto Joshua in Gilgal: and Caleb the son of Jephunneh the Kenezite said unto him, Thou knowest the thing that the Lord said unto

Moses the man of God concerning me and thee in Kadeshbarnea.

7   Forty years old was I when Moses the servant of the Lord sent me from Kadeshbarnea to espy out the land; and I brought him word again as it was in mine heart.

8   Nevertheless my brethren that went up with me made the heart of the people melt: but I wholly followed the Lord my God.

9   And Moses sware on that day, saying, Surely the land whereon thy feet have trodden shall be thine inheritance, and thy children's for ever, because thou hast wholly followed the Lord my God.

10 And now, behold, THE LORD HATH KEPT ME ALIVE, as he said, these forty and five years, even since the Lord spake this word unto Moses, while the children of Israel wandered in the wilderness: and now, lo, I am this day fourscore and five years old.

11 As yet I AM AS STRONG THIS DAY AS I WAS IN THE DAY THAT MOSES SENT ME: AS MY STRENGTH WAS THEN, even so is

**my strength now, for war, both to go out, and
to come in.**

**12 NOW THEREFORE GIVE ME THIS
MOUNTAIN, whereof the Lord spake in that
day; for thou heardest in that day how the
Anakims were there, and that the cities were
great and fenced: if so be the Lord will be with
me, then I shall be able to drive them out, as
the Lord said.**

Caleb said, "The Lord has kept me alive these 45 years.
I am now 85 years old, but I am still as strong today as the
day Moses sent me out. I'm just as vigorous and able to go
out to battle now as I was then. Therefore, give me my
mountain!"

Wouldn't you like to be as vigorous and strong at 85
as you were at 35 or 40? It doesn't matter how old you are.
Whether you're 30, 40, 50, 60, 70, 80, or older—if you call
on the Lord for your strength, you will be able to declare,
"Give me my mountain!"

Prayer Power

We couldn't say "Give me my mountain!" if we had to
rely on our own natural strength. But the Word tells us to
be strong in the Lord and in the power of His might.

EPHESIANS 6:10–18

10 Finally, my brethren, be strong in the Lord, and in the power of his might.

11 Put on the whole armour of God, that ye may be able to stand against the wiles of the devil.

12 For we wrestle not against flesh and blood, but against principalities, against powers, against the rulers of the darkness of this world, against spiritual wickedness in high places.

13 Wherefore take unto you the whole armour of God, that ye may be able to withstand in the evil day, and having done all, to stand.

14 Stand therefore, having your loins girt about with truth, and having on the breastplate of righteousness;

15 And your feet shod with the preparation of the gospel of peace;

16 Above all, taking the shield of faith, wherewith ye shall be able to quench all the fiery darts of the wicked.

17 And take the helmet of salvation, and the sword of the Spirit, which is the word of God:

18 Praying always with all prayer and supplication in the Spirit, and watching thereunto with all perseverance and supplication for all saints.

Ephesians 6:10 says, *"Finally, my brethren, be strong in the Lord, and in the power of his might."* Thank goodness, we don't have to be strong in ourselves. God didn't tell us to be strong in our own might. He told us to be strong in the Lord. We can lean on the everlasting arms of God. How? By communicating with our Heavenly Father—in other words, by prayer.

When I need an answer to something or am troubled about something, I pray about it. And after I pray, I always feel so much better. I feel so much stronger. Why? Because I've been communicating with my Heavenly Father, and I'm able to draw from His strength. In drawing from His strength, I become strong in the power of His might.

Notice that this passage in Ephesians starts by telling us to be strong in the Lord. Then it tells us to put on the armor of God, which is a logical transition. We start with "be strong" and transition to "how to be strong." What then does *prayer* (verse 18) have to do with it?

In this chapter, I want to focus primarily on verse 18, which tells us to pray always. As Christians, we are called to a lifestyle of prayer. The Lord has commanded us to pray at all times. First Thessalonians 5:17 tells us to pray without ceasing. Yet too often, we only pray when we need something from the Lord.

We use prayer as a means to call upon our "heavenly butler." We say, "Give me this! Hand me that!" Or we use prayer to call upon our "heavenly lifeguard": "God, save me! I'm drowning!" Yes, God is merciful and kind and He will save us when we are in trouble, but there is more to prayer than calling on a butler or lifeguard.

I quoted this passage before, but it bears repeating. First Corinthians 2:9 and 10 says, *"But as it is written, Eye hath not seen, nor ear heard, neither have entered into the heart of man, the things which God hath prepared for them that love him. But God hath revealed them unto us by his Spirit: for the Spirit searcheth all things, yea, the deep things of God."*

When we reach a deeper level in prayer, we will know and experience more of all that God has in store for us. Not only will prayer help reveal God's plan for our life, but prayer will also give us the strength we need to carry out that plan. Jesus said we would do the works that He did. How can that be possible? *Through prayer.*

JOHN 14:12–13

12 Verily, verily, I say unto you, He that believeth on me, the works that I do shall he do also; and greater works than these shall he do; because I go unto my Father.

13 And whatsoever ye shall ask in my name, that will I do, that the Father may be glorified in the Son.

Think of the many works that our Lord Jesus Christ did. Yet Jesus said that not only will we do the works He did, but we will do *greater* works! Have you ever stopped and let that revelation sink in? Jesus said that whatever you ask in His Name, He will do. What does the word "whatever" mean? It means *whatever*!

A Favor From Your Father

Now, in the natural, if you need to ask a favor of someone, whom do you ask? Do you ask a stranger? Not usually. Typically, when you need a favor, you ask someone with whom you have a relationship.

If I needed to borrow a car, I wouldn't ask a complete stranger for his car, and I wouldn't even ask someone I just barely knew and seldom talked to. I wouldn't feel comfortable asking a stranger, because I don't know him. Besides that, he might not *want* me to borrow his car.

So if I want to borrow a car, what am I going to do? I'm going to ask a friend of mine—someone with whom I have a relationship. I know it would be okay if I asked a friend for her car, because I know her; I have a relationship with her, and she would trust me to keep her car safe.

What if I needed some money? I'm going to ask someone with whom I've developed a relationship. I would feel comfortable asking her, knowing that if she had it, she would give it to me.

When my children were young, if I needed someone to take care of them, I asked someone I knew *very* well. It had to be someone with whom I had an even deeper relationship—and sometimes it was my niece, Candas, whom I asked. Why did I ask someone I was very close to? Because my children meant a lot to me, and I wanted them to be safe.

We all feel more comfortable asking someone we have a relationship with to do something for us—especially when it's someone who loves us and has offered to help us. And that's the kind of relationship we need to develop with our Heavenly Father—one in which we feel comfortable asking Him for whatever we need because we are that close with Him *and* because we know He loves us and has offered to give us whatever we ask for according to His will.

1 JOHN 5:14–15 (*Amplified*)

14 And this is the confidence (the assurance, the privilege of boldness) which we have in Him: [we are sure] that if we ask anything (make any request) according to His will (in agreement with His own plan), He listens to and hears us.

15 And if (since) we [positively] know that He listens to us in whatever we ask, we also know [with settled and absolute knowledge] that we have [granted us as our present possessions] the requests made of Him.

Verse 14 says we can have confidence, assurance, and boldness when we ask our Heavenly Father for something. We can feel that way because of the nature of our relationship with Him.

Again, in John 14:13, Jesus says, *"And whatsoever ye shall ask in my name, that will I do, that the Father may be glorified in the Son."* Whatsoever! We're limited many times in our natural relationships as to how much we can ask of our friends. But when we have a relationship with our Heavenly Father, we can ask the "whatsoevers."

It doesn't matter how big your need is. And it doesn't matter how small it is. What may be a small issue to you may be a big issue to someone else. And what may be big for you may seem small to another person. But whatever your need is, if the solution to your problem is promised in God's Word, then you can ask for whatever you desire, and it shall be done for you by your Father in Heaven!

When I ask my Heavenly Father for something in prayer, I stand on John 14:13, which says, *"And whatsoever ye shall ask in my name, that will I do, that the Father may be glorified in the Son."* Jesus said that! And Jesus cannot lie. So I'm not moved by any bad reports that may come my way concerning the situation I prayed about. I choose to believe Jesus instead of the bad report.

Sometimes in our walk of faith, we start being moved by the bad reports. But our faith must continually rest in God, confident that whatever things we ask in prayer, *believing*, we shall have them.

MARK 11:24

24 Therefore I say unto you, What things soever ye desire, when ye pray, believe that ye receive them, and ye shall have them.

Hey, God, Why Is It Taking So Long?

Whatever we ask for in prayer, *believing,* we shall receive. Just in case you didn't grasp John 14:13 (*"And whatsoever ye shall ask in my name, that will I do, that the Father may be glorified in the Son."*), Jesus added verse 14, *"If ye shall ask any thing in my name, I will do it."* He reinforces the truth so you would believe it: *If you ask anything in His Name, He will do it!*

If we really believed these passages on prayer that we have read, we would do a whole lot more praying! Ephesians 6:18 tells us to pray always. First Thessalonians 5:17 tells us to pray without ceasing. First John 5:14 and 15 says we can have confidence approaching God in prayer. John 14:13 and 14 tells us that if we ask anything in Jesus' Name, it will be done for us. And Mark 11:24 says whatever we ask for in prayer, believing that we receive it, will be ours.

Can you now see the importance of prayer? Prayer is a responsibility given to every believer. I've heard some people say they didn't have the "gift of prayer" and use that as an excuse for not praying.

We all have the gift of prayer. Yes, some people are gifted by God to lead people in prayer or instruct people on prayer. But every Christian has the basic gift of prayer; if we didn't, the Word wouldn't have commanded us all to pray!

Whatever God commands us to do, He gives us the ability to do. He has told us to pray without ceasing, so that means we are able to pray—and *should* pray! We just have to stir up that gift of prayer.

Stir Up the Gift!

My son loves my chocolate pie. When he asks me to make one, I first have to check to be sure I have all the ingredients in my kitchen necessary for making the pie. But I need more than ingredients. I can have the eggs, milk, cocoa, flour, sugar, vanilla, and butter—I can have all of those things in my kitchen. But until I gather all of those ingredients and combine them in the right proportions, they aren't going to do me any good. Even if I took them out of the pantry or the refrigerator and set them all on the counter, I'd still have to put them all in a bowl. But even if I made the effort to put them all in a bowl, they still wouldn't do me much good in the way of making a chocolate pie if I'm not willing to stir those ingredients. Without my stirring, those ingredients will never be transformed into a chocolate pie!

And I can't just stir one time, because chocolate pie filling is something that you have to keep stirring. If you don't keep stirring, the filling will be burnt, and you will have a chocolate pie that no one wants to eat. The whole time I'm making a chocolate pie, I stir that pie filling constantly. That's why I don't like to make it very often—because it takes a lot of time, effort, and attention.

Many Christians don't pray because of the time and effort it takes to keep stirring and stirring and stirring. But just as continual and consistent stirring helps make the most awesome chocolate pie around (according to my son), so continual and consistent prayer will yield awesome results in your life.

If you're not getting the results in prayer you want, take a look at the ingredients you have been using. Are you praying according to God's Word? Or have you mixed in some traditions of man or unscriptural ideas? Perhaps you aren't getting the results you want because you aren't stirring as much as you need to stir. It's so important to stir up that gift within you. When you start stirring up the gift of prayer, prayer becomes a way of life.

A Lifestyle of Prayer

I had a precious aunt who never married. When she got saved, she said, "I'm not going to marry. I'm going to dedicate my whole life to God and concentrate only on Him." And she did!

She was 95 years old when she went home to be with the Lord. And she lived her entire life as a praying woman.

If you didn't want an answer to your prayer, you didn't ask Aunt Oma to pray! Whatever she asked for, she received!

Prayer was such a lifestyle to her that she could not go a day without praying. Not only could she not go a day without praying, she couldn't go a day without praying *fervently*! She was a loud pray-er—that was just her style of praying.

I'll never forget one time when she was visiting me; she had been at my house for about three days when she said, "I have to go home, because I have to pray."

I said, "Aunt Oma, you can pray here."

She said, "I *have* been praying here, but I need to pray loud! And I can't pray that way when I'm here. I just don't feel comfortable to pray as loudly as I want to pray." She literally went home because she had to pray!

We need to get to the place in our prayer life where we don't feel right unless we've spent time in prayer. When we as Christians get to the place where we have a burning within to get down on our knees and touch Heaven, Heaven will open wide to each of us. God is calling for His children to be children of prayer.

When should we pray? Ephesians 6:18 says to pray at all times *The Amplified* says, "Pray at all times (on every occasion, in every season) in the Spirit, with all [manner of] prayer and entreaty. To that end keep alert and watch with strong purpose and perseverance, interceding in behalf of all the saints (God's consecrated people)." We need to pray at all times!

Does that mean we have to spend every waking minute with our head bowed and our eyes closed? No, it means we need to have a lifestyle of prayer. I know we live in a busy world, and we don't always have time to spend two hours on our knees praying. I realize that. Now there are times when we do need to spend concentrated amounts of time on our knees in prayer. But generally speaking, this verse is talking about living a lifestyle of prayer.

The problem with many people is, they are not living a lifestyle of prayer. They don't think about prayer or about communing with their Heavenly Father until there is a problem of some kind—*then* they hit their knees!

But we don't have to wait until there is a problem or even until we are on our knees. We can stay in an attitude of prayer throughout the day, which means we are spending our time thinking godly thoughts—ready and willing to hear God's voice whenever He speaks.

Before I go to bed at night, I pray. I thank God for giving His beloved sleep (Ps. 127:2). Then I confess according to God's Word, "Now I'm going to rest, and I'm going to sleep in the Lord." In the morning before I get up, I start praying and praising God, saying, "This is the day that the Lord has made; I will rejoice and be glad in it" (Ps. 118:24).

Do I always *feel* like rejoicing and being glad? No! But I start praying and building myself up. And as I've said, I play godly, faith-building music throughout my house 24 hours a day. That music helps keep me in an attitude of prayer.

When we praise our Heavenly Father, He opens His arms to us. He says, "My child, what do you want? Whatever you need, I'm ready to give it to you. Not only will I give you what you ask, but I'm ready to do exceedingly, abundantly above all that you can ask or think" (Eph 3:20).

Does your heart cry out to the Father? Do you desire to draw closer to Him and to commune with Him in a new and deeper way? Do you long for Him to talk to you and to show you His plan for your life? Prayer is the key. Through continual and consistent prayer, you will learn to hear His voice clearly. You will hear His directions on what to do and when to do it. Through a lifestyle of prayer, you will be able to walk in His ways, to do His will, and to draw closer to Him. I believe that a mighty fire is being stirred within you. Through prayer, those embers will soon explode into a mighty fire!

Remember, you are here on this earth for a reason. You are here for a special purpose. It's important that you take your place in God's great plan and not pull back. In order to go forward in the Lord, accomplishing what He has called you to do, you must make prayer a part of your lifestyle. It is your lifeline to God.

God is waiting to give you all that you need and desire. As you spend time with Him in prayer, building an intimate relationship with Him, you can ask whatever you will, and it *shall* be done for you!

Personal Prayer:

Father, may I be so stirred up that the spirit of prayer falls upon me, an anointing and an unction to pray like never before. May it come upon me in the morning, in the afternoon, and at night. May the burning desire to pray begin to spread in my home, in my friendships, and in my church. May that spirit of prayer strengthen me and enable me to stomp all over the devil, bringing down every stronghold and power of the enemy. Father, help me to march forward with the sword of the Spirit, with the Word of God. Teach me to pray and help me stir the gift of prayer until no obstacle can stand in my way. In Jesus' Name, I pray. Amen.

CHAPTER 10

Finding My Place Through Prayer

Prayer is vital to fulfilling the plan of God. Often God is limited in His ability to work in our life because of our lack of prayer. So it's important that we pray!

I've already given a brief history of how my annual women's conference came about. I want to share a bit more with you concerning how I found God's will for my life, one step at a time. God does not reveal the entire plan at one time, but He leads us one step at a time.

Sometimes it's difficult for me to divulge my personal thoughts and experiences, because I've always been one to keep them hidden in my heart. But I want to reveal some of my thoughts on this subject because I believe they can help you in your life today.

Where Do I Fit In?

Growing up, I was in the caught in a generational transition. Traditionally, "baby boomers" are those born between 1946 and 1964. I was born in 1945, just before the baby boomers, but at the end of a very different era. As a result, I often felt as though I didn't fit in.

To explain, in the 60s, young people (and some not so young), were rebelling against several outmoded traditions, one of which was the treatment of women and their role in society. On one hand, it seemed that women had no voice. The traditionalists felt that it was a man's world, and it wasn't really necessary for women to have a brain, because men would take care of everything for them.

On the other hand, women were rising up in protest to take their place . . . some were even saying they didn't need men for anything!

I didn't feel that either group was totally right. Because I was married and believed that marriage is an awesome calling, I didn't fit in with the rebellious group of the 60s.

But I also believed that God created both men and women for a purpose. He created women to have thoughts, desires, and dreams of their own, just as men do. And because I knew I had things on the inside of me to contribute to the world, I didn't fit in with the traditionalist group, either.

That was a tough season in my life, but as I sought God, I found my place and learned a valuable lesson. God has a purpose for you to fulfill, no matter what season of life you may be in. Ask Him to reveal His plan to you, and He will give you the strength to walk through that season with Him.

During the different seasons of your life, you get the opportunity to learn new things and develop new abilities. In fact, it was during my time as a stay-at-home mom that my prayer life developed.

What once was a frustrating time in my life became a precious time spent in God's Presence. My relationship with Him grew stronger and deeper and more intimate until I told Him with all honesty, "If prayer is my entire ministry for the rest of my life, I am committed to praying."

During those precious times, I prayed for my husband and for my children. I prayed for whomever and whatever the Lord brought before me, and it was during those times of prayer that my calling was truly birthed. I may have had glimpses of God's plan for my life at different times before, but the path on which I would walk out God's plan was laid through prayer.

You may prefer a 10-step formula that offers a quick solution, but if you truly want to know the fullness of God's plan for your life, *prayer is the answer*. Through prayer, you will discover your purpose and how to walk out that purpose in your everyday life.

Use Your Personality in Prayer

Each of us has natural gifts that can be powerful assets in prayer. Women tend to be more sensitive and attuned to what's going on around them than men are. Women are also very detail-oriented (unlike men who may not want to hear *every single detail* about the events of the day). Women like details!

Men tend to deal with problems this way: Okay, here's the problem. Do I have an answer? If I don't have an answer, I'll put the problem in my file drawer, close it, and forget about it for now because it's filed away. Women, on the other hand, rarely file anything away. We go round and round with that problem until we get an answer!

Some people would call a woman's tenacity "nagging." And while nagging can be a negative trait, I try to use my negative traits in a positive way. You see, it's okay to nag in prayer! Then it's not nagging at all. It's pressing on until we get the victory!

206

I was a stubborn child with a very strong will. As I got older, I learned to bring that trait under subjection and to allow God to use my personality for His glory. Now I am stubborn when it comes to prayer. I refuse to quit when I know something belongs to me in Christ. I have a strong will when it comes to fighting for the things of God!

Sometimes you have to fight your way through prayer. You have to be so stubborn that you refuse to give up when life gets hard. You have to be strong enough to say, "Satan, I don't care what you bring my way. I'm going to fight and believe and stand my ground until I win."

You Still Need to Be Wise

We have to be tenacious in prayer, but we also have to use wisdom. When a strong prayer movement began in the 1980s, progress was made. Things in the spirit world that needed to be dealt with were dealt with, and good results took place through prayer.

Then Christians moved so far into error that prayer and pray-ers got a bad reputation. People started doing ridiculous things in the name of prayer. Some women spent their entire day praying and fighting the devil, forgetting completely about their husband and children.

These women wreaked havoc in their homes. It went to the extreme of some women telling their husbands, "I can't have sex with you because I have to keep myself holy for the Lord." That's hogwash! It's even contrary to what the Bible says (1 Cor. 7:5).

Unfortunately, people got into error regarding prayer, and a lot of people got hurt. Ministers started backing away from prayer—the very thing that will take us where we need to go. Soon the enemy thought he'd won; he thought he had stamped prayer out of the Church.

But the devil is mistaken! Prayer is the power plant of the Church; it is vital for us as a corporate body and individually. Now is the time for the power of prayer to begin anew. You and I are going to be a part of that praying force. And we're not going to get into error, but we're going to join together as God intended.

What Should We Pray?

What should we pray? The Bible gives us many specific things to pray for. In addition to those commands, we can pray for anything that is backed by God's Word. We can also pray according to the leading of the Spirit, as He directs us to pray for certain people or situations. We can also pray in other tongues. Romans 8:26 says the Holy Spirit will help us when we don't know how or what to pray for with our own understanding or human intellect—in our own native languages.

Luke 6:28 tells us to pray for those who mistreat us. James 5:13 says to pray if we're in trouble. We are told to pray for people to be healed (James 5:16) and to pray for the peace of Jerusalem (Ps. 122:6). The Bible also tells us to pray that the Lord of the Harvest will send forth laborers into the harvest (Luke 10:2). And we're commanded to pray for all people and for those in authority over us (1 Tim. 2:1–3).

We have a responsibility to pray for the office of the President and our leaders, and we need to pray constantly, but especially when there are upcoming elections. Too many times, Christians don't even vote—much less pray! But your one vote can make a difference, and your prayers can too. Pray that the right men and women are elected to office. Pray that the person God wants as senator, congressman, governor, and so forth is elected. Pray that godly judges are appointed at every level.

We need to stand in the gap for our nation. Ezekiel 22:30 says, *"I sought for a man among them, that should make up the hedge, and stand in the gap before me for the land, that I should not destroy it: but I found none."* Let it not be said of us that God could not find someone to stand in the gap for our country.

Hey, God, Why Is It Taking So Long?

We must pray for our nation because we have a pivotal role to play in these last days. It's important that we keep our guard up through prayer, because the enemy wants to destroy us.

I want to share just part of a vision Brother Hagin had in September 1950. This vision is recounted in full in Kenneth E. Hagin's book *I Believe in Visions*.

> I saw the skyline of a large city. Looking closer, I saw the skyscrapers where burned-out hulls. Portions of the city lay in ruins. It was not written that just one city would be destroyed, burned, and in ruins, but that there would be many such cities. [1]

On September 11, 2001, the enemy struck a mighty blow against the United States. Since that attack, the 9/11 Commission discovered that the original plans called for several more American targets to be attacked—here at home and around the world. I firmly believe that it was because of prayer that the enemy was limited in his maneuvers.

On that fateful September day, this nation was wounded, but not destroyed. Don't think that marked the end of it. Now is not the time to become lazy in the area of prayer; we must keep a hedge of protection around our nation and around our families.

Pray for Your Natural and Spiritual Family

It's so important that we pray for our family. A nation is only as strong as her families. We also need to pray for the men of this country. There is a spiritual force coming against Christian men—a force such as I've never seen before. Satan knows if he can destroy the men, he can destroy the families.

Yes, both men and women have their part in these last days. The Lord showed me that it's going to take teamwork in these last days. It's only when we each take our God-given place and then work together as a team that we will be able to accomplish great things. Prayer changes things, so let's pray that both men and women will become the mighty vessels that God intends for us to be.

Lastly, we should pray *for each other*. We all have needs. We have desires that we want to see come to pass. You aren't alone in your walk with God. There are others around you who can support you and share this journey with you.

Other people in your church may go through the same things you go through. You can help each other along. Not only should we be fellow laborers in the Body of Christ, we should be friends. Lift up those around you.

Cry when they cry; rejoice when they rejoice. Encourage and strengthen each other—pray for one another.

James 5:16 says, *"Confess your faults one to another, and pray one for another, that ye may be healed. The effectual fervent prayer of a righteous man availeth much."* The *Amplified* says, "The earnest (heartfelt, continued) prayer of a righteous man makes tremendous power available [dynamic in its working]." There is tremendous power available to us in prayer, and the partnering with another person of faith in the prayer of agreement (Matt. 18:19) makes even more power available.

Partnering in Prayer

Although we can and should pray on our own, partnering with other strong Christians can add prevailing power to our prayer life and strengthen our faith. One example of the power of partnering in prayer is that of the great preacher Charles Finney.

The year was 1830; the place was Rochester, New York. The results: In one year alone, 10,000 people gave their life to Christ.[2] The reason could be attributed to Finney's prayer partner, Abel Clary. Finney once wrote, ". . . this Mr. Clary, and many others among the men, and a large number of women, partook of the same spirit, and spent a great part of their time in prayer. . . . This Mr. Clary continued in Rochester as long as I did, and did not leave it until after I had left. He never . . . appeared in public but gave himself wholly to prayer."[3]

There is power in agreement. Matthew 18:19 says, *"Again I say unto you, That if two of you shall agree on earth as touching any thing that they shall ask, it shall be done for them of my Father which is in heaven."*

When Should We Pray?

We know we need to pray and now we know *what* to pray, but *when* should we pray? You can pray when you wake up and while you get ready for the day. Pray in the shower or while you're getting dressed. Pray while you're driving in the car—just keep your eyes on the road! I pray when I'm driving, "Lord, help these other people drive!" (I'm just kidding!) But sometimes I do get so caught up in prayer while I'm driving that I miss my turns. You don't have to pray on your knees or in a prayer group in order for God to hear you. You can pray anywhere, at any time throughout your day.

If we want to obey the Lord's commands, we will pray. And contrary to what you might have thought or may have been taught, you can pray continually without getting weird or into error.

Hey, God, Why Is It Taking So Long?

Again, we should never pray to the neglect of our family. The Bible's command to "pray without ceasing" does not mean to pray twenty-four hours a day. Sure, there are seasons when we need to spend concentrated amounts of time in prayer, but generally, we can stay in an *attitude* of prayer throughout our day, praying as directed by the Holy Ghost.

For more detailed instruction on how to pray and what to pray for, I suggest reading Kenneth E. Hagin's book *The Art of Prayer*. It is very informative and discusses the different types of prayer we can utilize to accomplish great things for God's Kingdom.

Through prayer, you will bring into manifestation that which you have seen in the Spirit for so long. Through prayer, you are able to finally enter into that place to which God has called you. Don't lose the desire to pray. Don't lose that fervency but keep the fire inside burning ever so brightly. You will break through those unseen forces that have held you back and you will go forth into God's plan for your life as long as you keep that force of prayer alive in your heart.

Personal Prayer:

Heavenly Father, I'm going to keep this flame burning ever so brightly! I will not forget, Lord, what You are speaking to me. May it ever be written on my heart.

May I be reminded on a daily basis of the mission You have for me to accomplish. I commit this day to accomplish that mission. Lord, I will place You first in my life. I will honor You. I will keep my ears open to Your Word. And I will obey You in every area. God, I purpose to follow Your plan for my life. I will go forth with Your help and do what You've called me to do. In Jesus' Name, I pray. Amen.

---

[1] Kenneth E. Hagin, *I Believe in Visions* 2nd ed. (Tulsa: Faith Library Publications, 1984; 9th printing, 2002), 42–43. Citation is to the 9th printing.

[2] Basil Miller, *Charles Finney* (Minneapolis: Bethany House Publishers, 1941), 74.

[3] *Charles G. Finney, An Autobiography* (New Jersey: Fleming H. Revell Company, 1908), 297.

CHAPTER 11

Staying the Course

You may say, "Lynette, I used to pray about God's plan for my life, but so much time has passed, and those dreams haven't come to pass." Or you may say, "I wanted to follow God's plan and do great things with my life, but I have made too many mistakes. You don't know what I've done."

Psalm 107:1 says, *"O give thanks unto the Lord, for he is good: for his mercy endureth for ever."* God is forever merciful. When we trip up—when we mess up—God is merciful. He doesn't treat us according to what we deserve. He gives us mercy! And that mercy can rewrite our life's story.

Romans 10:17 says, *"So then faith cometh by hearing, and hearing by the word of God."* When it comes to the Word of the Lord, the more we read it and the more we say it, the more it gets rooted on the inside of us. Sometimes, our minds are slow to comprehend. Sometimes our hearts are not open to receive. But once we get it—once we truly get hold of what God is saying to us, nothing can stop us! When the revelation of the Word enlightens our heart and mind, we will do great things for the Lord.

No matter what you have or have not done in the past, God's mercy is available to you. God still has a plan for your life. So receive God's mercy and forgiveness, and forgive yourself. Choose to continue on with God's plan.

When we get off course in life, it may take some time to find our way back. Even though getting back on course is an option, it's better to stay close to God all along.

Staying in Touch With God

Several verses in First Corinthians chapter 2 give us some insight into the importance of staying in touch with God.

1 CORINTHIANS 2:9–11 (*NIV*)

9   However, as it is written: "No eye has seen, no ear has heard, no mind has conceived what God has prepared for those who love him"

10 but God has revealed it to us by his Spirit. The Spirit searches all things, even the deep things of God.

11 For who among men knows the thoughts of a man except the man's spirit within him? In the same way no one knows the thoughts of God except the Spirit of God.

Notice the last part of verse 9: "what God has prepared for those *who love Him*." When you love someone, you like being around him, right? You want to fellowship with him and talk with him. You want to spend time with him.

Sometimes I wonder what God must think about us. We say we love Him. We're always asking Him for something. But how much do we fellowship with Him? How often do we talk to Him just to be talking to Him and spending time with Him?

Imagine a natural family—one set of parents and two children, for example. Imagine that the children grew up in the home with the parents, but after they became adults, they left home and moved to another state. What if those children never went back home to visit their parents, and the parents never went to visit the children? Even though they are the same flesh and blood, after a period of having no fellowship whatsoever, what's going to happen? Those parents and kids aren't going to be as close as they once were. They won't understand each other as much as they once did, because they haven't been communicating with each other. They're not even going to be thinking along the same lines—all because they haven't been fellowshipping on a regular basis.

So many times a similar thing happens with God's children. We get saved and filled with the Holy Spirit, and we think we have it made. We know we're going to Heaven and that God loves us, and, eventually, we drift away to do our own thing and live our own life. We gradually stop fellowshipping with our Heavenly Father.

How important it is to fellowship with God! James 4:8 says, *"Draw nigh to God, and he will draw nigh to you...."* When we draw near to our Heavenly Father, He draws near to us. And, as I said, the closer we draw to Him, the better we are able to hear His voice.

If you're not receiving clear direction from the Lord, check up on how close to Him you're walking. Are you drawing near to God?

Check Up on Your Armor

Many times we wonder why we're being defeated. We wonder why our prayers are not getting answered. We need to check up on our relationship with God, and we need to check up on our armor. How much armor are we wearing?

EPHESIANS 6:10–11

10 Finally, my brethren, be strong in the Lord, and in the power of his might.

11 PUT ON THE WHOLE ARMOUR OF GOD, that ye may be able to stand against the wiles of the devil.

Ephesians 6:11 says, *"Put on the whole armour of God, that ye may be able to stand against the wiles of the devil."* We can't just wear one piece of armor or half the armor and expect our life to function as it should. The Word didn't say to just put on *part* of our armor. It says to put on the *whole* armor of God so we can stand against the wiles, or devices or schemes, of the devil. That means if we *don't* have on the whole armor of God, we *won't* be able to stand against the wiles of the enemy.

We can't just put on part of the armor—the part we like—and expect to be equipped to be fully victorious in life. You see, there are some parts of the armor that we like better than others. Some are easy to put on and some are a little bit heavier! Some parts of the armor may feel cumbersome and it takes more commitment to wear them. Often the problem is that we just want to wear the parts of the armor we like.

But what does the Word say? It says to put on the *whole* armor of God. Why? So that we are able to stand! If you've been having trouble standing, check up on your armor. Have you put on the whole armor or just parts of it? We need all of it if we want to stand against the attacks of the enemy.

The enemy is mean! He doesn't follow any rules, and he doesn't fight fair. That's why it's so important that we put on the whole armor. We can't just put up our fists and fight, because this is not a physical battle. This is a spiritual battle, and we must have our spiritual armor on if we're to win.

If we're going to follow God's plan for our life, there will be attacks against us. There will be warfare in the heavenlies and activity in the spirit realm that we will have to come against. Don't think that the opposition you face in this world is natural opposition. Don't fall into the trap of blaming other people for your struggle to find and fulfill your destiny. The Bible tells us that we aren't wrestling against flesh and blood. But the Bible does say there will be wrestling!

EPHESIANS 6:12

12 For we wrestle not against flesh and blood, BUT AGAINST PRINCIPALITIES, against POWERS, against THE RULERS OF THE DARKNESS OF THIS WORLD, against SPIRITUAL WICKEDNESS IN HIGH PLACES.

This spiritual battle is fiercer than any natural battle you have or will ever experience in your lifetime. Don't think life will be a bed of roses and that walking out God's plan will always be easy. You're going to come against these things mentioned in Ephesians 6:12. There is an enemy who does not want you to fulfill the plan of God for your life. The Bible says he is seeking to devour and coming to steal, kill, and destroy (1 Pet. 5:8; John 10:10).

Fight the Good Fight of Faith

With the full armor of God on, you can and will be victorious if you will stay the course and continue to fight the good fight of faith!

First Timothy 6:12 says, "Fight the good fight of the faith. Take hold of the eternal life to which you were called when you made your good confession in the presence of many witnesses" (*NIV*). We know what the fight of faith is.

But so many times we get tired and weary of fighting. Then the enemy comes in and tries to discourage us. He tells us, "See, that faith stuff doesn't work. Look at all the battles you're having. Look at what's happening in your life! This wouldn't be happening if that faith stuff really worked."

No, my friends, faith *does* work. But it takes time and patience. There is a spiritual battle going on right now, and if we want to win, we must persevere. We must *continue* to fight the good fight of faith!

When you decide to follow the plan of God for your life, whether you're in full-time ministry as a vocation or in some other field such as finance, politics, the arts, education, and so forth, you're going to wrestle against principalities and powers of darkness. The enemy wants to see if you're truly committed to following God's plan to the end. He wants to know if you will still stand your ground when darkness assails and it looks as if God has forgotten you.

EPHESIANS 3:13

13 Wherefore take unto you the whole armour of God, that ye may be able to withstand in the evil day, and having done all, to stand.

With Christ on your team, you're never a loser. And as my husband always says, *you cannot be defeated if you will not quit*! So when the storms of life come your way, just keep on keeping on. Keep your eyes on the finish line—on the plan of God for your life. *You can make it!*

In the midst of great battles, remember that these are opportunities to experience great victories, because great victories come from great trials. That's why it's so important to keep our eyes on the prize and focus on the finish line.

Many people want to have a good testimony. But you can't have a good *testimony* without some *tests*! Tests and trials are going to come to us all. But we have the assurance that God will be with us and that He will see us through to the other side.

In the midst of trials and tribulations, it's easy to take our eyes off what God has called us to do. Sometimes we start looking at what our brother or sister is doing. We begin to think, *So-and-so never has any problems! Why is life great for them and not for me?*

Why? Why? Why? The enemy would love for us to get caught up in the mental realm of trying to reason things out and always asking why. We don't need to ask why; we just need to trust God. Don't envy your brother and sister when things are going well for them. Just praise God for what is happening in their lives and rejoice that they're experiencing victory. Then if they're having trials and tribulations, pray for them.

We need to bind together and pray for one another instead of envying and back-biting one another. We need to get rid of the spirit of competition. There shouldn't be any competition in the Body of Christ, because we're supposed to be working toward the same goal and for the same purpose: to win the lost to Christ and to bring back the King!

Do you know why there have been so many tests and trials lately in the Body of Christ? The enemy wants to see if you believe what you say you believe. He's trying to do everything he can to deter you from fulfilling God's plan for your life. But your life has a divine purpose; there is a calling of God upon your life! So keep your eyes focused on that call.

Focused on the Finish Line

It was many years ago that the Lord revealed a definite plan for our ministry. He gave us a definite path for our life. But it took many years for those plans to come to pass. In the meantime, we had to stay faithful to the calling. We had to be faithful to obey God and to trust that He would bring His plans to pass. Even when it seemed as though they might never come to pass, we had to believe that things would be just as God had said they would be.

I remember when much of the plan was revealed to us. It was years ago, shortly after my husband, Ken, and I moved to Oklahoma to begin working for Kenneth Hagin Ministries.

We were staying with my mother-in-law and father-in-law and were spending the night in one of their spare bedrooms. Ken had fallen asleep, but the spirit of prayer came upon me. (I've learned that if the spirit of prayer comes upon you, it's crucial that you yield to it and *pray*.)

So I began to pray very quietly in tongues and suddenly began to interpret in English what I had been saying in tongues. At the time, this was kind of new to me, because I had interpreted my prayers only a couple of time before that.

Later Ken told the story this way. He said, "I was sleeping and suddenly heard this booming voice. I recognized it as Lynette's voice, and my first thought was, *Oh, my goodness. My wife is hollering so loud, she's going to wake up the whole house*! I turned to try and quiet her down when I realized she was in fact praying very quietly, like in a whisper."

That night came in the midst of a particularly trying time for both of us. We were both a little discouraged because we did not know our purpose for moving to help Brother Hagin in his ministry. We had been in full-time ministry back in Texas, where Ken was an associate pastor and had been ministering in the pulpit each week. Then the Lord suddenly told us it was time to move and to go another direction in the ministry.

The Lord directed us to Kenneth Hagin Ministries, which was based in Tulsa, Oklahoma. My husband's new job entailed not one single "pastoral" duty (such as preaching, ministering to the sick, counseling church members, and so forth). The job entailed being in charge of Brother Hagin's meetings. And that meant taking care of the entire behind-the-scenes administration, setting up sound systems, catching people in prayer lines, setting up chairs—anything in the natural that you could possibly imagine that needed to be done, and nothing spiritual whatsoever.

My husband is a preacher and has always been a preacher. One of the things I've always loved about him is that he can preach! But he wasn't preaching at all during that season of our lives. And on top of everything else, his salary was cut in half! In the natural, it looked like a demotion. As I said in a previous chapter, people around us thought we had missed it. But in the Spirit, we knew that the change was right.

However, sometimes even when you're doing what you know you're supposed to do, your head can still give you problems. When your head starts giving you a problem, the enemy comes along to join right in. He starts telling you that you missed God and made a mistake and that you were better off before. But if you will be sensitive to the Lord on those "down" days, He will minister comfort to you and lift you up.

So as I prayed, I began to interpret what the Lord was saying to us to comfort us. Plans came out of my mouth that I didn't believe were even possible, much less likely. They were things I'd never dreamed of or hoped for! I was so shocked that I could hardly deliver what I was saying, because I certainly wasn't believing for anything like that to ever come to pass.

Yet those things did come to pass, but not overnight. The plans God gave to us didn't come to pass in 5 years or 10 years or even 15 years. In fact, many of them are just now coming to pass today.

During those many years when it seemed as though God's plans would not come to pass in our life, we had opportunity after opportunity to take our eyes off the goal. We had numerous opportunities to look to the right and the left. But we knew that we were following the plan of God for our life—and that alone is what kept us going.

When you follow the plan of God for your life, there will be challenges. There will be times that your mind will give you fits. In those times, you must be as a race horse and wear blinders, so to speak. Put blinders on so that you're not tempted to look to the right or to the left. Then you won't be tempted to wonder why your accomplishments don't equal someone else's accomplishments—why you aren't running your race as fast as someone else is running his. Instead, you will keep your eyes on the finish line and complete the plan of God for your life.

We must learn to be satisfied with God's plan for our lives and to rest in His plan. His plan for our life is better than any plan we could devise. He knows what will make us truly happy, and He longs to brings those things to pass in our life. We just need to let Him.

Following God Step by Step

Have you ever had another person say something to you and it not come to pass? For example, they said they were going to do a particular thing for you, and then they didn't do it. It hurts, doesn't it? You may have felt disappointed or let down.

As a minister of the Gospel, it bothers me when ministers lose their credibility. We need the world to believe what we say so that they will believe the Gospel we preach.

Therefore, I don't like for a minister to say something and then it not come to pass.

Time and again, I've heard ministers say, "We're going to do such-and-such," but then it never takes place. I understand that many times, things come up or circumstances change, and what was originally planned just doesn't happen in the way the person thought it would. But people still lose their confidence in that person. Sometimes the sheep are scattered; church members leave the church.

This tendency bothered me so much that I once asked the Lord about it. I said, "How can we avoid saying things that we then can't or don't follow through on?" I'll never forget what He told me. He said, "Let Me unfold the plan before you reveal the plan."

Let Me unfold the plan before you reveal the plan! In other words, we can still put forth vision. We must have vision. But it's important that we give out the vision that the Lord gives and that we give it out one step at a time—until the vision becomes clear.

What if you're not a minister? You still need to have a vision, or goals, for accomplishing what God has planned for you. But you have to take it step by step, letting God unfold His plan to you in full before you begin telling others about it. If something has been laid upon your heart and keeps stirring on the inside of you, just let it keep stirring. But don't reveal it; don't speak it out to anyone until you have clear direction as to exactly what you're supposed to do to accomplish it.

If 30 years ago when God first spoke to us, we had focused on the *end* of His plan instead of walking out His plan one step at a time, we would have missed the end result. We would not have been able to do what we are doing now.

Too many times we try to jump from step 1 to step 5. We want to bypass all the steps in between. Then we want to jump from step 5 to step 10. But that's not how God has planned it. He has planned for us to take one step at a time. So focus on what God has for you to do *right now*.

I received the following prophetic utterance from the Lord as I ministered at *Winter Bible Seminar 2004*.

> . . . *You've begun to question, "Why God?*
>
> *Why has it not worked as I thought it would work?"*
>
> *It's because you've looked to man's plans instead of to My plan.*
>
> *You've tried to take many steps at a time, but I say to you,*

Walk out the plan that I have for you. . . .

Some of you have to get back.

You've gotten off course so much.

You have to get back. You have to get back to the very basics. . . .

And as you get back to that, as you fall on your face before Me,

Asking me, "The plan, the plan, the plan,"

I will reveal the plan that I had planned for you from the very beginning.

Yes, those things that were in your heart! Yes, they were right!

But you started looking over here and over there and all around you,

Searching for the tools to implement that plan instead of seeking My face—

Instead of being patient and letting it come to pass in My time.

But as you get back on course, there'll be a time of rejoicing.

Where there have been tears, there shall be rejoicing!

Oh, yes, for a great plan awaits! A great plan awaits!

Hey, God, Why Is It Taking So Long?

And you shall reach many; many shall come into the
Kingdom.

Your heart has been right, but you've looked to the
wrong source.

Now get back to Me. Get back to Me to hear My voice....

Have you been searching for answers to the questions you have? The Lord wants to speak to you. As you commune with Him, as you focus on Him, you will be enlightened. You will hear clearly the answers you long for.

As you allow God to guide you, you will walk out His plan. You may have said, "I'm not qualified. I can't do it." But you can, because you aren't going in your strength or in your own power or might. You're going in the strength, power, and might of the Lord!

God wants to do greater and greater things in our lives, but we must draw near to Him. We must worship Him. And as we are diligent to seek God's face, He will be our steady guide and continual source of comfort, strength, and wisdom in every area of our life.

CHAPTER 12

Turning Stumbling Blocks Into Stepping-Stones

Sometimes after being inspired in our faith, we think there isn't any mountain that we can't move. But when the mountain of trouble, so to speak, really does appear in front of us, it's a different story altogether.

It's important to understand that the faith walk is not a walk of ease. It's not always fun to endure life's problems, but James 1:4 tells us to let endurance have full play, or let it run its full course. We would probably rather go through life on "flowery beds of ease." But that's not the way life works. We are living in an imperfect world with imperfect people, and life is not going to be easy all the time.

JAMES 1:2–4 (*Amplified*)

2 Consider it wholly joyful, my brethren, whenever you are enveloped in or encounter

trials of any sort or fall into various temptations.

3 Be assured and understand that the trial and proving of your faith bring out endurance and steadfastness and patience.

4 But let endurance and steadfastness and patience have full play and do a thorough work, so that you may be [people] perfectly and fully developed [with no defects], lacking nothing.

According to James, it's important to understand that faith will never grow without it being tried and proven. In this life, there are going to be trials of your faith. But in all those things you must, as James said, "count it all joy" (v. 2). The *basis* of faith is the Word of God, and the *proof* of faith comes from living a *life* of faith.

As Christians, we must live that life of faith. Our faith will be tested, and it will be tested more than once. It's not like going to a class and being tested just three times and then passing the course.

No, our faith is going to be tested again and again and again throughout life. I know you may not feel like shouting about that fact, but if you will understand it, you will be able to shout *in spite* of whatever comes your way.

God never promised that the Christian life would be free of tests, trials, and adverse circumstances. But He did say in Psalm 91:15, *"He shall call upon me, and I will answer him: I will be with him in trouble; I will deliver him, and honour him."* And Isaiah 43:2 and 3 gives us similar assurance.

ISAIAH 43:2–3

2 **When thou passest through the waters, I will be with thee; and through the rivers, they shall not overflow thee** [you're not going to drown in those trials!]: **when thou walkest through the fire, thou shalt not be burned; neither shall the flame kindle upon thee.**

3 **For I am the Lord thy God, the Holy One of Israel, thy Saviour. . . .**

When we hold on to God in the waters of adversity, we have His promise that we're not going to drown. It doesn't matter if you can't swim, because the Lord is going to hold you up in that water. He said He'd be with you, and He won't let you drown!

As we saw in Chapter 6, our Heavenly Father wants us to learn to totally rely on Him. So many times we want to do everything in our own strength. We want to say, "Okay,

God, just give me the courage and show me what to do, and *I'll* do it." In other words, *we* want to fix the situation.

But we need to learn to say, "God, this situation is out of my control. I tried to fix it, but it didn't work. And now I don't know what to do. My idea wasn't the right idea. Father, I was wrong; I thought I knew what to do. I thought I would try to help You, but I failed." When we do that, then God is able to come in and *really* fix the situation.

What God wants us to do is to come to Him in a test or trial and completely trust in Him. Jesus said, *"Come unto me, all ye that labour and are heavy laden, and I will give you rest"* (Matt. 11:28).

Unshakable Faith

You must base your entire life on your faith in your Heavenly Father. Everything around you may fall, but if you will hold on to His hand, He will hold you up in the midst of every storm.

It's a fact that Satan wants to destroy you. We've already seen that the enemy goes about as a roaring lion seeking whom he may devour (1 Peter 5:8). He's trying to shake your trust and confidence in God. He's trying to get your eyes on your problem. And he's yelling in your ear,

"See, your God is not delivering you. Your God is not here. What happened to your God?"

But we need to be like the three Hebrew children—Shadrach, Meshach, and Abednego—who said, "Our God will deliver us, but even if He won't, we're still going to serve Him" (Dan. 3:17–18). We must have that same kind of unshakable commitment behind our faith.

So many times, we only want to serve God because of what He's done for us and the fact that He has blessed us. But we must determine to serve God regardless of whether we're blessed or not. When you make that kind of commitment, the blessings of God will certainly be yours.

Now what do we do when life brings problems our way? What should be our response? There is a saying, "When life gives you lemons, make lemonade." Lemonade is pretty good—add a little sugar to it, and it's wonderful!

That's what you have to do—make lemonade! You can become victorious by taking whatever life brings your way, going to God with it, and allowing Him to turn it around for good.

The Bumps Are What You Climb On!

I'm reminded of a story about a little boy who was leading his sister up a mountain path. The way was not easy because it was rocky and bumpy. So finally, the little girl said, "Brother, this isn't a path at all! It's all rocky and bumpy!" To this her brother replied, "Sure, Sis, the bumps are what you climb on!"

Right now, you may be reading this and laughing to yourself as you think, *I have so many bumps in my life—that must mean I'm going to climb high!* Well, you probably are. The enemy likes to put large bumps in the way of those he is afraid are going to be a success for God.

So if you're having mammoth trials today, I want to encourage you. I want you to know that you are very special to God! Don't allow the enemy to destroy you before you finish your race!

Instead of allowing the bumps to become stumbling blocks, use them as stepping-stones! That's the attitude that I've always tried to take in my own life concerning problems. It's the attitude that says, "Yes, there are bumps, but I won't allow them to cause me to stumble. I'm going to keep stepping higher, and higher, and higher!"

You can triumph over the bumps in your life. I've never seen a successful person who didn't have bumps in his life. You may look at a successful person and think, *Well, they've just got it made.* But you don't know all the trials that he went through to get where he is today.

No one is immune to the bumps of life. If you're going to be a success in life, you must understand that the road is going to be rocky and bumpy at times. And you must remember that you can climb on those bumps to get to the top.

Everyone is going to have bumps in life. The Bible is full of stories about people who faced difficulties. Abraham is a good example of someone who had many tests of faith in his life. What did he find as soon as he arrived in Canaan—the land God had promised him? There was a famine!

You may have thought that you reached your promised land, and then, suddenly, there was famine in your life! Well, I want to encourage you to hold on, because the last chapter has not been written in the book of your life!

Then Abraham had trouble with his relatives. (Does that sound familiar?) And when war came to Canaan, Abraham had to fight in battle. (Maybe you feel as though you're on a battlefield today.)

Then on top of that, Abraham received bad advice from his wife and was led down a wrong path. Ishmael was born as a result of her counsel, and the situation brought great sadness into Abraham's life. But when Abraham and Sarah got back on the right track, the promised son Isaac was born, and there was great joy.

Perhaps at that point, Abraham thought, "Oh man! I've got it made now. I went over a few bumps, but I've made it to the top now, and my promised son Isaac is here." But then God told Abraham, "Sacrifice Isaac; give him to Me" (Gen. 22:2).

Give God Your All

While God isn't telling any of us to sacrifice our children, He is saying to us, "Give Me your all." Yet so many times Christians hold back and don't give everything to Him. But we need to be willing to give Him our all. Notice that God did not require Abraham to kill Isaac. All He required was a willingness. Similarly, we, too, must let go and say, "Okay, God, whatever You say—I'm willing to obey."

As far back as I can remember, I always knew that I was called to the ministry. But at first, I only wanted to do what *I* wanted to do in the ministry. I wanted to be a pastor's wife. I thank God I am now, but years ago, it wasn't that way. At that particular time in God's plan, He had something else for me to do.

So many times Christians try to plan out their lives for God. But it's important that we let *Him* plan our lives. It wasn't until I was in my lowest depths that I came to the place where I said, "God, I'm going to quit trying to plan my life and let You plan it for me."

You see, I always thought that I had committed my life to Him, but I had only committed *most* of my life to Him. There was a little reserve that I kept for myself. And, finally, when I committed to Him 100 percent, He began to lead me on a path that I would have never dreamed could have come to pass. I can't tell you that it's been smooth sailing all the way. No, there have been many bumps in the road. But God has taken me through every one of them! Not *some* of them, but *every one* of them!

It's so important that you say, "Okay, God, I'll give You 100 percent." Maybe you have been fighting it. Maybe things have not been going right in your life because you haven't committed your whole body, soul, and spirit to your Heavenly Father.

You have never experienced the kind of peace you will experience when you commit your whole heart to the Lord. He will give you a peace that passes all understand-ing—a full and complete peace. And it does not matter what circumstances come your way or what bumps come your way, because you will know that you're holding on to the hand of the One Who will get you through every cir-cumstance that comes your way. You will know that you can't go under for going over, because your God is present. And because you will have committed everything to Him, you will know that He is there to deliver you out of every adverse circumstance of life.

Climb Over Your Circumstances

Joseph is another example of someone who had to walk a path full of bumps and rocky places. He began his life as his father's favorite, but he was hated by his brothers, and they sold him as a slave. Then Joseph was falsely accused of a crime and thrown into jail. There he was seemingly forgotten and forsaken, but he eventually rose to be the second in command of all of Egypt.

Like many people in the Bible, Joseph didn't quit. Instead, he took the stumbling blocks in his life and used them as stepping-stones to climb the mountain that stood before him.

I don't know what bumps may be in your path right now. But I'm telling you that I know what it's like to want to give up. I know what it's like to say, "God, how much more can I take?" But when that happens, I go to a promise in the Bible. The following verses are from one of my favorite passages in the Bible, Psalm 91.

PSALM 91:11–12

11 For he [God] shall give his angels charge over thee, to keep thee in all thy ways.

12 They shall bear thee up in their hands, lest thou dash thy foot against a stone.

Notice that God doesn't promise to remove every obstacle from your path, but He does promise to help you overcome them as you turn the stumbling blocks into stepping-stones. And He promises to help you climb higher *in spite* of life's bumps or problems.

The difficulties in life will enable you to climb higher and higher if you'll use them as stepping-stones. However, too often, we only want to complain about them. Sometimes we may try to kick them out of the way or jump over them. Or, more often, we try to go around them. But when we finally get around one, there's sure to be another bump in our path!

When facing these bumps in life, it is easy to want to turn around and go another way. But, thank God, as a Christian you don't have to quit or give up, because you can turn stumbling blocks into stepping-stones!

When circumstances come in your life, I want to encourage you to just get up on those stones and say, "I am more than a conqueror through Christ Jesus [Rom. 8:37].

Hey, God, Why Is It Taking So Long?

Greater is He that is in me, than He that is in the world [1 John 4:4]." Then go to the next stone and say, "I'm standing on the promises that cannot fail! When the howling storms of doubt and fear assail, by the living Word of God I shall prevail—standing on the promises of God!"[1]

When you get to the next stone, your body might be racked with pain or weakened by a serious disease. But get on that stone and say, "My God has delivered me. He has healed me. By His stripes I am healed" (Ps. 34:19; 1 Peter 2:24). And if fear is surrounding you, get on that stone and say, "God has not given me a spirit of fear, but of power, and of love, and a sound mind" (2 Tim. 1:7).

Whatever the circumstance is in your life, find a promise in the Word of God concerning the situation, confront your problem and say, "I cannot go under for going over. I am standing on the Rock—the Rock Christ Jesus—and He will put me over."

Friends, that's how you climb over the circumstances. Adverse circumstances come against every one of us. And they don't just come one time, but they are going to come again and again.

Continuing to ask "why?" will defeat you every time. I alluded to the fact previously that asking "why" when tests and trials come only hinders us from defeating those trials and walking in our victory. Maybe you can't get over the circumstances of life because you've been questioning, *Why, God? Why me? I've stood on Your Word. I've prayed. I've lived life as well as I knew how. Why is this happening to me?*

The Lord wants us to stop questioning Him and to start trusting Him. He wants you to know that He will bring you through *every* situation in your life. Stop spending your time questioning the circumstances, but use those circumstances as bumps you can climb on.

Start turning your stumbling blocks into stepping-stones today by finding scriptures in the Word of God that deal with whatever circumstances you are facing. Then begin to "step" on each stone according to the Word of God until you climb higher and higher and are victorious in Christ Jesus! Start praising the Lord right now for victory over whatever stumbling blocks are in your life!

The "bumps"—or problems—in life don't have to be troublesome stumbling blocks that continually hinder your progress. Instead, you can use the bumps as *stepping-stones* and climb to the place God has destined for you one step at a time!

---

[1] R. Kelso Carter (1849–1928), "Standing on the Promises."

CHAPTER 13

Commitment Plus Contentment Equals Joy

When we face various trials—or bumps—in life, there is a temptation to lose our joy. Circumstances often threaten to steal our contentment. But we can learn to be content, no matter what is going on around us and no matter where we are along God's path for our life.

One subject we don't hear taught very often, but desperately need to hear about, is the subject of contentment. In the day and age in which we live, discontentment seems to be prevalent not only in the world, but in Christian circles. We know the reason non-Christians are discontented: true joy, peace, and contentment are only found in Christ. But as I have traveled and counseled with many people, I have found that more and more Christians are not content.

Hey, God, Why Is It Taking So Long?

One person who knew the secret of contentment was the Apostle Paul. In writing to the Philippians, he shared his secret of contentment even while he was enduring imprisonment, chains, and bonds. However, from the attitude Paul portrayed when writing the letter to the church at Philippi, those reading it would not know he was experiencing adverse circumstances.

PHILIPPIANS 4:4–13

4 Rejoice in the Lord always: and again I say, Rejoice.

5 Let your moderation be known unto all men. The Lord is at hand.

6 Be careful for nothing; but in every thing by prayer and supplication with thanksgiving let your requests be made known unto God.

7 And the peace of God, which passeth all understanding, shall keep your hearts and minds through Christ Jesus.

8 Finally, brethren, whatsoever things are true, whatsoever things are honest, whatsoever things are just, whatsoever things are pure, whatsoever things are lovely, whatsoever things are of good report; if there be any

virtue, and if there be any praise, think on these things.

9 Those things, which ye have both learned, and received, and heard, and seen in me, do: and the God of peace shall be with you.

10 But I rejoiced in the Lord greatly, that now at the last your care of me hath flourished again; wherein ye were also careful, but ye lacked opportunity.

11 Not that I speak in respect of want: for I have learned, in whatsoever state I am, therewith to be content.

12 I know both how to be abased, and I know how to abound: every where and in all things I am instructed both to be full and to be hungry, both to abound and to suffer need.

13 I can do all things through Christ which strengtheneth me.

This passage contains words of victory, joy, encouragement, and love. Yet Paul faced adverse circumstances while writing this letter. In my own experience of traveling to Rome and visiting the ancient dungeons and prisons, I can only imagine some of the difficult circumstances under which Paul wrote his various prison epistles. There is no place to use the restroom, no light, no fresh air, and barely room to move. Yet he said, "I have learned to be content in whatever state I'm in."

Paul knew the secret of living a satisfied life. He was *contented*, because he was *committed*. A good equation to remember is this: *Commitment plus contentment equals joy.*

Paul wrote that letter to the Church at Philippi because they had sent him gifts to cheer him up. He told them, "I appreciate the gifts of cheer, and I appreciate your remembering me while I'm here. I'm thankful that you have done this, because you're going to receive the rewards that I'll receive [Phil. 1:5–7; 4:17]."

Paul went on to say, "But I am not dependent upon these things. Whether or not you sent these gifts, I would be content, for I depend on God and His strength."

Many times, we become dependent upon the things God provides for us instead of being dependent solely upon God Himself. When we look to God for our strength and joy and not just for the blessings He gives, we will be content, regardless of our present circumstances or possessions.

A Living Example for Christ

Discontentment will cause us to lose our Christian testimony. Many Christians have lost their joy and are no longer an example to the world. Who wants to become a Christian if it means losing one's joy? Non-Christians are already discontent. Why would they want to become a Christian if all they see are discontented Christians? If we aren't content or full of joy, how can we expect to win others to Christ?

My dad always told me to be a *living* example to those around me. It's easy to talk the talk. It's easy to tell someone, "God loves you. You ought to serve Him." But it's much harder to display that God-kind of love. For some people, their Christian witness is all words. The Bible says that faith without works is dead (James 2:20). We have to add some *action* to our words.

I never have to look for an opportunity to witness for Christ. Opportunities always come to me because I endeavor in everything I do to be a living example for Christ. I believe that if we display Christ-like characteristics, other people will approach us. We won't have to ask them if they know Christ; they will ask us about Him!

Characteristics that catch people's eye are joy, peace, and contentment. Everyone is looking for more joy and peace in life. In the troubled world in which we live, peace outside of Christ is impossible to find. And everyone wants to be content. It's hard to meet anyone who is satisfied with his or her life. So if you are full of joy, peace, and contentment, you will stand out wherever you go!

'Preach the Gospel—If Necessary, Use Words'

I frequented a particular carpet store for more than a year, making multiple purchases throughout that time. I tried to display the love of God each time I went in the store, but I hadn't had an opportunity to minister the Gospel with words. One morning, that all changed.

It was the morning I went to the store at about 8:30 a.m., which was very uncharacteristic of me. But I walked in there as I always did—bubbly and full of joy.

(Each day, when I leave my house, I say, "The joy of the Lord is my strength." And if it wasn't for the joy of the Lord, I could never make it, because it's His joy that gives me the strength to accomplish all I have to do in a day.)

When I walked in there that day, it was the first time the employees had seen me that early in the morning. I usually went shopping closer to noon, because I'm a night person and as I jokingly say, I'm not fully awake before noon! The owner was surprised to see me and said, "Lynette, you sure are in here early this morning. It's shocking to me that you still have that same smile on your face that I see every time you're in here. A lot of people come in here, but not all of them smile the way you do. Every time you walk in here, there is such joy that flows through you. You must know something I don't know."

I said, "Yes, I do! You see, the love of God flows through me, and it's through Him that I can have joy. Through Him, I have peace and contentment."

Because of my consistent godly example that stood out from the way other people lived, I was eventually able to share the Gospel with the owner of the store. I didn't have to approach him. He approached me, wanting to know why I was happy all the time!

We should always strive to be living examples of Christ-like character, and we won't have to make opportunities to minister to others; opportunities will come to us. Remember that your very countenance, whether a frown or a smile, is a testimony of your life. Choose to smile!

Don't misunderstand me. It's not that we're never going to have any problems; it's that we know our help comes from the Lord. And the Lord told us not to worry or fret, because He would supply all of our needs (Phil. 4:19). We must take God's Word literally. That's what faith does.

We have to take the Lord at His Word when He says not to worry or fret about anything and that we can do all things through Him (Phil. 4:6,13). Many people say those verses with their mouth, but few really believe it in their heart and live it out in their life. Therefore, they are not content. They do not have joy, and they are never satisfied in life. If we could solve life's problems, we already would have. We can't do it ourselves, so why worry about it? Faith believes that *God* will do it.

I'm reminded of the story about a man who was having financial problems. He had tossed and turned all night, worrying about the situation when scriptures began crossing his mind: "Do not be anxious about anything [Phil. 4:6]. God will supply all of your needs [Phil. 4:19]" He was then reminded of the scripture that says God never slumbers or sleeps (Ps. 121:4). This man chose to take God at His Word and said, "Lord, I'll tell You what. There's no use in both me *and* You staying up, so I'm going to sleep."

That's how all of us should be when it comes to taking God at His Word. Believe what He says! That's the key to having joy and being content.

True Contentment Defined

In Philippians 4:11, Paul said, *"I have learned, in whatsoever state I am, therewith to be content."* Some people may think a statement like that shows a lack of ambition. They think it means the person isn't willing to try to rise above the bad situation. But Paul wasn't lacking ambition. He probably accomplished more in one day than some people will accomplish in a lifetime.

The Greek word translated "content" means self-sufficient, sufficient for one's self,[1] and in context, carries the connotation of *to be master of the situation.* God wants us to be victor of the situation; and to be conqueror of circumstances. How negative does that sound? I'd say it's pretty positive!

So what Paul wrote to the Philippians was something like this, "Regardless of the situation I find myself in, I have learned to be master of the situation. Regardless of the circumstances around me, I have learned to conquer the circumstances. I have learned to be victorious, no matter what comes my way."

Paul knew what true contentment is. To be master of one's circumstances—no matter what those circumstances are—is one of life's greatest victories. Too many times, we allow our circumstances to be master over us.

There are many famous people in this world who would not have done the great things they did if they had allowed their circumstances to master them. One such person that comes to mind is football legend Rocky Bleier.

Not falling within the ideal of what a running back should look like, Bleier had to run harder and play smarter to be able to stand out. Despite his drive and ability to make the big play, the Pittsburgh Steelers only considered him a late round pick. But before the season ended that first year, he was drafted again . . . this time by the United States Army. At the height of the Vietnam War, Bleier was thrust into combat early and was seriously wounded when his platoon ran into an ambush. Receiving wounds from both rifle fire and grenade fragments in his legs, he was barely able to walk and his professional football career seemed to have ended before it began.

For more than two years, he drove himself. Little by little he overcame obstacles and fought his way back. He not only made the Pittsburgh Steelers, but also eventually became a starting running back on a team that won four Super Bowls and became the greatest football team of the 20th century.[2]

After being told he'd never walk normally again, much less play football, Bleier became master of his circumstances and did not allow his circumstances to master him. He learned to walk and went on to become one of the best football players to ever play the game.

If someone tries to tell you that you'll never make it, don't let their opinion about you shape your opinion about yourself. Keep fighting the good fight of faith, believing that the dreams God has put within your heart will indeed come true.

How to Uproot Discontentment

A discontented person can make himself and everyone around him miserable. How it must grieve God to see His people so discontented in life, especially when He sent Jesus to give us abundant life (John 10:10).

Whenever I visit other countries, I'm reminded how blessed we are to live in the United States of America. Conveniences we take for granted and view as necessities are considered luxuries in other parts of the world. We are fortunate to live in a land of plenty, a land of opportunity, where if someone is willing to work for a dream, anything is possible.

If you want to more greatly appreciate your country, go visit another country. It's no wonder people love to come to America. I never really realized how much a privilege it was to live here until I began visiting other nations.

We tend to think the grass is greener on the other side, but if you don't learn to be content where you are right now, you won't be content on the other side either!

Discontentment is like a weed; you don't have to do anything for it to grow. If you allow it to be planted in your heart, it will grow on its own. You don't have to water it or nurture it, it'll just grow.

It takes effort to be content. We have to learn it and practice it. It's only achieved through continual application and sustained effort. By going to school, so to speak, we can learn to be master of our circumstances.

You might say, "But, Lynette, you don't know what my circumstances are. If you were in my shoes, you wouldn't be content either. You don't know the person I'm married to or the trouble my children have caused me."

Everyone has some issue in his life that could give him reason to become discontented. None of our lives are free from problems, but it's how we approach the problems that count. Whether we approach them negatively or positively will determine whether we are contented or discontented. The key to being victor over our circumstances is to approach each circumstance in a positive way.

Step One: Be Committed

Of course, the first thing we must do in order to be contented is to be committed. To whom or to what are we supposed to commit? We are to be committed to Jesus

Christ. The Bible makes it clear that our devotion to God ought to be first and foremost.

MATTHEW 6:33

33 But seek ye first the kingdom of God, and his righteousness; and all these things shall be added unto you.

PSALM 37:4–5

**4   Delight thyself also in the Lord: and he shall give thee the desires of thine heart.
5   Commit thy way unto the Lord; trust also in him; and he shall bring it to pass.**

You will never be completely happy in life until you have committed your entire self to the Lord. You will never know true contentment until you have committed your life to God.

Today it seems that a commitment is the last thing anyone wants to make. People say, "Don't get too close to your mate; don't commit too much, because he [or she] might disappoint you." But commitment is very important in every area of life.

If I had an indictment against the charismatic movement, it would be that there's a lack of commitment among its members. I've seen many charismatics leave a church they had been committed to because they wanted to have more freedom of expression. But then they never committed to another church after leaving the first one.

Many Christians just drift from church to church, refusing to become a member or to take an active part in any one of them. They say it's because they don't want to be in bondage, but some people use that term as a cop-out. What many people call bondage is actually commitment. People don't want to commit to teaching a Sunday School class, because they may want to go fishing or sleep in next Sunday.

People don't like responsibility. But life is full of responsibility. And it's important to learn how to be committed and how to stay committed.

ROMANS 12:1–2

1   I beseech you therefore, brethren, by the mercies of God, that ye present your bodies a living sacrifice, holy, acceptable unto God, which is your reasonable service.

2   And be not conformed to this world: but be ye transformed by the renewing of your mind, that ye may prove what is that good, and acceptable, and perfect, will of God.

MATTHEW 16:24

24 Then said Jesus unto his disciples, If any man will come after me, let him deny himself, and take up his cross, and follow me.

The Lord requires commitment of us. He requires us to offer our body as a living sacrifice and to be transformed by the renewing of our mind. It takes *a lot* of commitment to not be conformed to this world. It takes commitment to take up a cross!

As I write this book, I am now a pastor's wife, but I first shared this message on commitment and contentment in 1981—when I was still an evangelist's wife. Ken was still on the road traveling. RHEMA Bible Church didn't even exist. But we were content because we were committed to following God's plan for our life, no matter what it was.

Commitment isn't easy, but it's rewarding. When you make the *commitment*, *contentment* follows. And not only are you contented, you are enabling the Lord to do just what He said He would do. And you will be confident of that fact. As you seek first the Kingdom of God and His righteousness, all the other things are added unto you. When you make an unconditional commitment to God, He sees to it that you are rewarded. You will begin to see the results of your faith, and you will discover that commitment is the key to contentment.

Would You Serve God if There Were No Rewards?

Remember the commitment of the three Hebrew young men. Shadrach, Meshach, and Abednego when they said, "Our God is able to deliver us, but even if He wasn't, we still wouldn't serve your god." They were committed, regardless of what happened. That's how much they trusted the Lord.

We need to be so committed that regardless of the circumstances, we will still serve the Lord. Too many people have the attitude, "God, if You bless me, I'll serve You." Or, "God, prosper me, and I'll witness for You." But that's not the way it goes.

I'm reminded of President John F. Kennedy's famous speech when he said, in effect, "Ask not what your country can do for you—ask what you can do for your country." I like to apply that philosophy to our Christian life: "Ask not what God can do for *us*; ask what *we* can do for Him."

I'm certainly not saying we shouldn't ask God for anything, but too many times we're so intent on what the Lord can do for us, that we forget about what we can do for Him. We must remember to ask God, "What can I do for

You?" One reason people are so discontented is that they are constantly looking out for their own needs instead of looking to meet the needs of others.

Someone who always thinks of himself and what he can get will never be content. That person may think the only way to reach contentment is to look out for number one, so to speak. But we must give of ourselves in order to be contented. It is truly more blessed to give than to receive (Acts 20:35).

When it comes to giving, I've always had a very good example to follow. My dad was a very giving person. Over the years, I have seen him give and give and give. I watched him stay at a hospital all night long so he could minister to people. I saw him miss meals or eat cold meals because he was busy reaching out to others. Many times, he gave his own money to those in need, and he always gave his love.

My dad never expected anything in return when he gave. Sometimes the reason we don't reap a reward on our giving is because we only gave in order to get a return. If you give only to get, you're not really giving. It's still self-ishness. But when you give freely, not expecting anything in return, you will be blessed in your giving and, in fact, receive a return. God's laws of sowing and reaping do work when we follow them with a pure motive.

I observed at an early age that true happiness and contentment come from giving to others. Giving truly brings a sense of satisfaction and a joy that we will never experience otherwise.

The Secret of Contentment: Enjoy *Today*

Many people don't enjoy their present success because they are constantly thinking of ways to become an even greater success. Regardless of what you are doing right now, be the best you can be. And be content, enjoying each success as it comes. Don't always wish for tomorrow; learn to enjoy today.

Have you ever heard the phrase, *Tomorrow never comes*? In other words, each day you live is always "today." Even when tomorrow rolls around, it won't be tomorrow when you're living it; it will be *today*. Don't become so wrapped up in the future that you miss out on today. Yes, you can have aspirations and ambitions. But learn to be content with what you have and what you are right at this moment. Give today your best, and give the rest to God.

I see so many people discontented in their job. They cannot enjoy the job they have right now, because they are thinking of the possible promotion they might get in the future. So many people can't enjoy their home right now, because they're thinking of the better home they're going to get in the future. Yes, let's reach for success, but let's also enjoy what we have right now.

Many times, parents of young children think, *I'll be so glad when they get a little older.* But enjoy your children while they are young, because that age only lasts a little while and then it's gone forever.

I have visited the home of newlyweds and have complimented them on their home. Their house was small but lovely. And they said to me, "You ought to see what we have planned for the future." Their response made me want to cry, because I realized that unless they learned the secret of being content where they were, they wouldn't be content no matter how big their next home was.

I'll never forget our first home. It wasn't a very large house. It was an old house; in fact, it was so old that the windows were rotting out. When the cold north wind blew, it was easy to become discontented. There were times we had every burner on the stove turned on, because without central heat, that was the only way we could warm the house. And we still had to get under electric blankets to stay warm!

But I was always content there. There was love in that home, and that's the most important thing to have in a home. It doesn't really matter where you live or how big the house is; it's what's inside the house that counts. I knew that house wasn't the end, but the beginning. I knew I hadn't reached my ultimate goal, but I also knew I could enjoy that part of my life's journey. If I could enjoy that success, more successes would come. And they did.

Some of our friends moved into better homes before we did, but I never once got jealous. Many times we will miss what the Lord has in store for us by becoming jealous of someone else's success. Jealousy is a sure way to hinder our blessing.

Be thankful for what that other person has; rejoice with him or her over what he or she has received. And be content with what you have, knowing that your time will come if you'll continue to stand on the Word. When you are content with your present state and when you stay faithful to do what you're supposed to do at the moment, the Lord will surely reward you.

You can learn to be content regardless of what you have. You can learn to be content with much as well as with little. As you gain more success, don't constantly think of the future; be happy where you are right now.

The secret to being content regardless of your present state is to know that God will take care of you. When you know that He will meet your every need, your needs won't bother you! Why? You are content, knowing that God will take care of them. When we place God first in our life and seek Him above all else, everything we need will be added unto us. When we delight in the Lord, He gives us the desires of our heart (Ps. 37:4). And when the desires of our heart are met, contentment and happiness follow.

We often become discontented because our daily tasks sometimes seem mundane and unimportant. When the desires and dreams in our heart seem to go unfulfilled, it's very easy to become discontented. We must remember that God has not forgotten us—or the dreams in our heart. And when we stay faithful to follow God's leading in the "here and now," He will see to it that our future needs are met and our dreams fulfilled.

'But, Lord, I Can Do *More*!'

I'll never forget when God told me it was time for me to minister only to my family. It was the hardest thing I ever did. As I said, I never had difficulties with commitment, but as it turned out, it was only because I was doing what *I* wanted to do. When the Lord told me to do something I didn't particularly want to do, it was hard to obey!

Now I've never been one to neglect my family. I've never neglected my husband or my children. If anything, I neglected myself, so that I wouldn't neglect others. But as

Hey, God, Why Is It Taking So Long?

Ken began to build RHEMA, the opportunity for me to minister to other people disappeared.

Up until that time, I had been involved in actively ministering to others. I was involved in counseling, helping in church services, playing the piano for praise and worship, working the crusade book table, and so forth. Then the Lord said, "It's time for you to minister just to your husband and children." And it was the hardest thing He ever asked me to do.

I did not mind ministering to them, but I wanted to do more. Can you relate? Do you feel like there is so much more you want to do with your gifts and talents—so much more you *can* do? So many times we want to minister to the "world," but the world is sitting right in our home. Unless we can be a success there, we won't be a success anywhere else.

Many children are being neglected because parents are more concerned about winning the lost than winning their own families. If we gain the whole world and lose our own family, what have we really gained? Success begins with the family. It doesn't matter how big a ministry or church is—or how big a career becomes—a successful person is one with a successful family.

But it was difficult for me to adjust to being at home all the time instead of out ministering to people. I had always been around people, and I love people! Years ago, I worked as a hairdresser, and you know how hairdressers are around people all day long. It was a great opportunity for me to minister. I never knew how many problems women had until I started doing their hair every week!

The Lord told me, "It is time for you to train your children and to minister to your husband." And there I was at home 24 hours a day. My world revolved around a one-year-old and a five-year-old. It wasn't much fun to feel as though my vocabulary consisted of gibberish. Sometimes at night I would go to the grocery store just to see people and have adult conversation!

I could have very easily become a basket case, and I almost did! Then I learned Paul's secret. *Commitment plus contentment equals joy.*

One morning, I gave myself a stern talking. I said, "Look, Lynette! You cannot change these circumstances. You know that this is definitely what the Lord told you to do. Since you can't change the circumstances, you're the one who has to do the changing." *I* finally did the changing and became contented. I became victor and master and conqueror of my circumstances.

Are you discontented because you don't want to do what God has called you to do at this time? Do the dreams in your heart tug at your mind and cause you to become discontented in your present situation? It's only as you become content with what God has planned for you at *this* time that promotion will come.

Promotion comes from the Lord as we are faithful to obey what He has told us to do. After faithful obedience (and sometimes a lot of patience!), our due season will arrive, and we will reap the promised reward. Galatians 6:9 says, *"And let us not be weary in well doing: for in due season we shall reap, if we faint not."* God will promote you to the place He has planned for you if you are careful to follow Him each step of the way.

The Difference Between Teaching and Training

This section is devoted to parents of younger children, but it can bless and help anyone, no matter what your status or season of life. Childhood is such a brief but important time. No one can teach your children the things of God like you can. Proverbs 22:6 says, *"Train up a child in the way he should go: and when he is old, he will not depart from it."* Some parents wonder why the Word isn't working in their child's life. One reason may be that they didn't really *train* their children.

Did you know there is a difference between teaching and training? Someone can teach you about typing all day long, but until they actually show you where the keys are and sit beside you while you learn the keys yourself (going over it again and again if you make mistakes or ask questions), you're never going to successfully learn how to type. The same thing is true when it comes to training your children. You can tell them what is right all day long, but until you live it out before them and show them a godly example, they aren't going to remember what you *said*—only what you *did*.

Training takes more time and effort and patience than teaching. *Showing* children how to do something takes more time than just *telling* them how to do it. You have to be more hands-on and involved to *train* your children.

I remember the neighborhood kids always came over to our house to play. I wanted them there so I could influence them. A neighbor called me once to ask me why her child had come home singing a certain song. She said, "When my son comes home from being at your house he is full of such peace and joy. What do you do over there, anyway?" I told her we always played Christian music in the house.

The way you train your children will affect them for the rest of their life. Their early years are very important. Instead of neglecting them, we can guide them along the right path, and they will not depart from it when they are grown.

Training your children and ministering to your family takes commitment, especially if you have other dreams in your heart. Remember, God's timing is just as important as God's plan. The Bible says, *"To every thing there is a season, and a time to every purpose under the heaven"* (Eccl. 3:1). I encourage you to nurture the dreams in your heart through prayer and time spent with God. If it is taking longer than you would like, be patient. Rely on Him to make all things beautiful in their time (Eccl. 3:11).

When you commit your life to God, don't commit 80 percent or 90 percent—not even 99 percent. Commit yourself to Him 100 percent. The Lord will help you set your priorities and keep them in the right order so you won't neglect Him or your spouse or your children or your calling. But you must keep your priorities in order.

You see, God never asks you to do something that will hurt your family or cause damage to other people. Keep your priorities straight: God, spouse, children, calling. When you stay faithful to what the Lord requires, He will make it up to you with great reward—both spiritually and naturally.

I encourage you to cling to Christ, to lean on Christ, because through Him you can be conqueror of your circumstances. Romans 8:37 says, *"In all these things we are more than conquerors through him that loved us."* When you experience the immense love God has for you, you are able to be content no matter what is going on around you. No matter what your circumstances are, you are more than a conqueror through Christ who loves you. When you are committed to God and contented in Him, then *"God shall supply all your need according to his riches in glory by Christ Jesus"* (Phil. 4:19).

God is El Shaddai—the One who is more than enough. He is the All-Sufficient God, and He will do all that He has promised to do. He will supply all of our needs if we will seek Him first. Learn to commit to Him. Learn to be content in Him. And He will give you joy unspeakable every day of your life.

---

[1] Joseph Thayer, *Greek-English Lexicon of the New Testament* (Grand Rapids: Zondervan Publishing House, 1977), 85.

[2] Rocky Bleier, Inc., "His Story," http://www.rockybleier.com/story.html. Reprinted by permission.

CHAPTER 14

The Blessings of Waiting Upon the Lord

I believe a new day is dawning in your life. The Lord is doing a new thing in your heart as you commit yourself to Him. And I believe you are closer than ever to discovering and fulfilling His plan for your life.

First Corinthians 2:9 says, *"But as it is written, Eye hath not seen, nor ear heard, neither have entered into the heart of man, the things which God hath prepared for them that love him."* This verse is referencing an Old Testament passage found in Isaiah chapter 64. Most people who quote this verse in First Corinthians stop with verse 9. But the passage continues in the next few verses, and those verses that follow are very important.

1 CORINTHIANS 2:9–11

9   But as it is written, Eye hath not seen, nor ear heard, neither have entered into the heart

of man, the things which God hath prepared for them that love him.

10 But God hath revealed them unto us by his Spirit: for the Spirit searcheth all things, yea, the deep things of God.

11 For what man knoweth the things of a man, save the spirit of man which is in him? even so the things of God knoweth no man, but the Spirit of God.

According to verse 9, we have not seen with our eyes or heard with our ears, nor has it entered into the heart of man what God has prepared for us. Standing alone, that verse would leave us feeling helpless to find God's plan for our life. But verse 10 tells us how we are to discover God's plan. It says that God has revealed it to us by His Spirit! Hallelujah!

We must be willing to listen to the Holy Spirit if we want Him to reveal to us the plan of God for our life. It's so important that we follow the plan of God for our life and follow it explicitly. The only way we can follow that plan is to listen to the voice of God. And the only way we can listen to the voice of God is by communing with our Heavenly Father.

It may help you to reread the chapters on prayer to help encourage you to spend that vital time communing with the Lord. Remember, He won't reveal His full plan to you all at once. You discover each part of the plan through prayer. If you don't continue in prayer on a regular basis, you will only know part of God's great plan.

It's so important that you don't stop short of what God has for you. He has so many good things in store for you. As you trust Him to direct your paths, those good things shall be yours.

PROVERBS 3:5–6

5 Trust in the Lord with all thine heart; and lean not unto thine own understanding.

6 In all thy ways acknowledge him, and he shall direct thy paths.

Proverbs 3:5 says to trust in the Lord with all your heart. It's impossible for you to follow the plan of God for your life if you don't trust Him. If you truly want to follow His plan for your life, you have to develop such a trust in Him, lean on Him to such an extent, and commune with Him so intimately that you have full confidence in Him. You have to be confident to the point where you absolutely, beyond any shadow of doubt, know that whatever He tells you will indeed be performed and come to pass exactly as He has said.

The path you were created to take may not be the path you had in mind. The path I thought I would take is not the path I took at all! But in a way, it's been fitting for me. I've always preferred to travel by back roads instead of by highways, so I could enjoy the beautiful scenery. Well, God has definitely taken me on the scenic route in my life! It seems that on my life's journey, I've been on back roads and winding paths and around some corners that overlooked deep valleys. I'm telling you, I felt afraid to look down! But the most important thing I ever did was determine that I was going to trust in the Lord with all of my heart.

I made the decision to never question the path He led me down. Sometimes I wanted to question and ask, "Why is this happening? God, this doesn't seem like the plan You had for me." But I had determined to trust in the Lord with all of my heart, regardless of the path I was taking. My confidence was in the Word of the Lord, and I believed He was bound to perform that which He had promised.

There were times when I had to play a certain David Ingles song over and over. The song says, "My confidence is great in the Lord."[1] I played that song over and over and over again until the words lodged deep in my heart, and I truly believed them.

There may be times when you have to hear an encouraging message or scripture over and over again. Why? Because your head will try to get in the way of your heart. Hearing the Word over and over will strengthen your spirit, train your mind, and help you stay strong in your beliefs. It will help you remain determined and committed to walk God's path and to believe that He will perform what He has promised.

Do you trust in the Lord with all of your heart? Have you come to the place in your life where you are acknowledging Him in all your ways? Have you stopped leaning on your own understanding and begun leaning on the understanding of the Lord?

His ways are so much higher than our ways. And His thoughts are so much greater than our thoughts. So we must trust in the Lord with all of our heart and lean not to our own understanding. When we do that, He *will* direct our path. We can count on it!

You Can't Move Forward Looking Back

As I said, continually camping on the "whys" when tests and trials assail will defeat you. In my own life, I finally came to the place where I said, "God, I'm not going to question You. I'm not going to waste my time asking questions any more, because there are more important things I need to hear from You than an explanation for something that has already happened."

You can't go forward if you're always looking backward. In fact, in the natural, it's dangerous to try to move forward while you're still looking backward! You could get hurt doing that; you could fall over an edge or crash into something.

Sometimes we become so focused on looking at what has happened in the past that we can't enjoy what God has for us right now, in the present, and we can't press on to what He has for us in the future. It's time to follow the example set by the Apostle Paul and *press on*!

PHILIPPIANS 3:12–14 (*NIV*)

12 Not that I have already obtained all this, or have already been made perfect, but I press on to take hold of that for which Christ Jesus took hold of me.

13 Brothers, I do not consider myself yet to have taken hold of it. But one thing I do: Forgetting what is behind and straining toward what is ahead,

14 I press on toward the goal to win the prize for which God has called me heavenwards in Christ Jesus.

You can't do anything about the past by looking behind you, and you certainly can't do anything about the future while looking behind you. What's behind you is behind you, so fix your eyes on the goal set before you and press onward!

Hurry up and Wait!

Galatians 6:9 says, *"Let us not be weary in well doing: for in due season we shall reap, if we faint not."* In a previous chapter, we learned that it's only after our faithful obedience and lots of patience that our "due season" arrives. Hebrews 6:12 says that we inherit the promises of God through faith and patience. We know there are waiting seasons in life. We know we must be patient and wait for God's timing. But what does it mean to "wait upon the Lord"?

Isaiah 40:31 says, *"They that wait upon the Lord shall renew their strength; they shall mount up with wings as eagles; they shall run, and not be weary; and they shall walk, and not faint."* We tend to focus on the parts of that scripture that we want to see—and that's the "flying as eagles" part, the "running and not growing weary" part, and the "walking and not fainting" part. We don't focus enough on the part that is the actual key to receiving the other parts we so want to experience.

Hey, God, Why Is It Taking So Long?

In reading Isaiah 40:31, we focus on the fact that the Lord is going to renew our strength. We're tired, so we quote this scripture, believing for the Lord to renew our strength, to help us mount up with wings as eagles, and to help us to run and not be weary. But what is the prerequisite for all those wonderful things to take place? What condition must first be met? The beginning of the verse says, *"They that wait upon the Lord . . . ."*

We tend to think that "waiting on the Lord" means basking in His Presence, and that is certainly a part of waiting on the Lord. We need to spend time in the Lord's Presence. When we are in His Presence, we are built up and strengthened. And we are then able to run and not be weary.

But the Lord has shown me that there is another aspect of waiting upon Him. And that is the aspect of being patient while He reveals His plan for our life in His perfect timing. You see, God's plan for our life does not happen overnight. There is a waiting process that can last for years as we wait for God to shape us, and as we wait for God's plan to take shape.

Of course, we don't like to go through the waiting process. We'd rather go from step 1 to step 50, all in the same day. "Wait" is not a word we like to hear—whether it's said in a restaurant when we want to be seated at a table right away, or by our spouse when we're ready to leave for church. We don't like to be stuck in traffic or in a line at the grocery store. We want answers to problems as immediately as we want our microwave popcorn!

But God says, "They that *wait* upon the Lord . . . ." There are times when the best thing we can do is wait, but we must wait *upon the Lord*. We have to stay prayerful and committed while we wait for His plan, in His way, in His time.

Waiting on the Lord means being patient when your life doesn't seem to be panning out the way you thought it would. It means trusting that the Lord's plan *will* come to pass. Waiting on the Lord means spending time with Him on a consistent basis, praying, listening, and getting to know Him. It means waiting until the Lord says, "*Now.* Now is the time!"

As I said, in too many areas of life, we don't want to wait. A lot of young people are in a hurry to get married; they don't want to wait. Then after they marry, they want to immediately possess what it took older married couples 40 years to accumulate.

For nearly everything in life worth having, there is a waiting period. There is a proving time and a molding time. We don't like to go through those times because they can be painful and hard to bear.

Sometimes I think most women can tolerate waiting a little better than most men can, simply because women who are mothers have learned how to be patient from taking care of their children. As any parent knows, it takes patience to be a good parent! And because childrearing is often more the woman's responsibility than the man's, women are sometimes more inclined to wait. But all of us have to learn to be patient and to wait on the Lord.

Waiting on the Promise

As much as we don't like to wait, it's something everyone has to do. Even the Lord's disciples had to wait to receive God's promise.

ACTS 1:1–7 (*NIV*)

1 In my former book, Theophilus, I [Luke] wrote about all that Jesus began to do and to teach

2 until the day he was taken up to heaven, after giving instructions through the Holy Spirit to the apostles he had chosen.

3 After his suffering, he showed himself to these men and gave many convincing proofs that he was alive. He appeared to them over a

period of forty days and spoke about the kingdom of God.

4   On one occasion, while he was eating with them, he gave them this command: "Do not leave Jerusalem, but wait for the gift my Father promised, which you have heard me speak about.

5   For John baptized with water, but in a few days you will be baptized with the Holy Spirit."

6   So when they met together, they asked him, "Lord, are you at this time going to restore the kingdom to Israel?"

7   He said to them: "It is not for you to know the times or dates the Father has set by his own authority."

Isn't this just like us? The Lord tells His disciples to wait and to not leave Jerusalem until they've received the Promise. But they aren't able to obey His command without question. They want to know when He plans to restore the kingdom to Israel. And what does Jesus tell them? He says, "It is not for you to know the times or dates the Father has set by His own authority." In other words, He tells them to wait.

Hey, God, Why Is It Taking So Long?

Many Christians get so involved trying to interpret prophecies. One of the big ones is to discover when the Lord is coming back. There have been so many different dates predicted (all of them wrong). Why do people bother? The Bible says that no man knows the day or the hour of the Lord's return (Mark 13:32). It makes no sense to spend time trying to figure out when Jesus is coming back.

Most Bible prophecies take a long time to be fulfilled. When we try to interpret them, we do so using only the knowledge we have at the moment. Therefore, we often misinterpret what the Lord is saying.

You may have had prophecy spoken over you, and you have been busy trying to make it come to pass instead of waiting upon the Lord. Don't neglect what you could be doing today by trying to fulfill something some person said about you.

Don't Mistake Man's Prophecy for God's Plan

We know that each one of us has a calling upon our life. Whatever your calling is, it will be revealed to you by the Spirit of the Lord. Remember the passage we read at the beginning of the chapter?

1 CORINTHIANS 2:9–11

9   But as it is written, Eye hath not seen, nor ear heard, neither have entered into the heart of man, the things which God hath prepared for them that love him.

10 But God hath revealed them unto us by his Spirit: for the Spirit searcheth all things, yea, the deep things of God.

11 For what man knoweth the things of a man, save the spirit of man which is in him? even so the things of God knoweth no man, but the Spirit of God.

You may receive a prophecy that *confirms* something the Holy Spirit already spoke to you, but don't focus so much on what someone else says that you neglect to hear the voice of God for yourself.

My husband and I have a dear friend who was frustrated because a so-called prophecy he received didn't seem to be coming to pass in his life. This man sincerely wanted to follow the plan of God for his life, so when someone prophesied to him that he was called to ministry, he actually considered leaving his profession and entering full-time ministry.

Yet for some reason he couldn't do it. This man grew frustrated concerning the prophecy because he wanted to do what God wanted him to do, yet he didn't feel in his heart that he should leave his business (he was a very successful businessman).

Finally, he talked to Brother Hagin about it. Brother Hagin realized that this man had understood the prophecy to mean pulpit, or full-time ministry, and explained, "That prophecy doesn't necessarily mean you're called to pulpit ministry. You can be called as a businessman to hold up the hands of ministers."

That revelation set this man free! And he and his wife have done a superb job of supporting ministers and ministries. They've been the most wonderful cheerleaders anyone could have. They're continually cheering my husband and me on.

In the Old Testament, Aaron and Hur weren't called to the ministry the way Moses was, but Moses would never have fulfilled his destiny without the two of them doing what God had called them to do (*see* Exodus chapter 17). It's so important that we each take our place.

Busy While We Wait

In Acts chapter 1, Jesus gave His disciples instructions and told them to wait for the baptism in the Holy Spirit.

Jesus knew they needed this power from Heaven in order to take their place and fulfill their mission on earth.

ACTS 1:8 (*NIV*)

8   But you will receive power when the Holy Spirit comes on you; and you will be my witnesses in Jerusalem, and in all Judea and Samaria, and to the ends of the earth. . . .

The disciples waited in Jerusalem just as Jesus commanded. But they didn't just sit on the couch and wait, nor did they go about their daily business in town. Verse 14 tells us what they did while they "waited."

ACTS 1:14 (*NIV*)

14 They all joined together constantly in prayer, along with the women and Mary the mother of Jesus, and with his brothers.

While the disciples waited, they were *constantly in prayer*. Of course, they didn't know exactly what they were waiting for. Jesus had simply said, "Stay in Jerusalem until you are endued with power from on High." They didn't know what this "power from on High" was, but they waited, anyway. And while they waited, they prayed—*constantly*.

Hey, God, Why Is It Taking So Long?

What better thing to do while we wait for God to reveal His plan! Through prayer, we can develop such a relationship with the Lord that we will easily recognize His will and His plan.

Waiting upon the Lord means that even when God reveals the plan, we don't expect it all to take place instantly. Not only will prayer enable us to recognize God's voice when He gives us the plan, but through prayer, we can also learn *when* and *how* God wants the plan to take place.

I've already shared in previous chapters how I became frustrated when I didn't see God's plan coming to pass according to my timetable. In 1972, the Lord revealed various things He had in store for Ken and me—things we are just now doing. Of course, I wanted to do them back in 1972!

Several years passed without the plans coming to pass. Finally, I began praying to God about it—mainly out of frustration. One thing He told me during my time in prayer is that I would someday lead others in prayer. Well, that wasn't anything I desired to do. So I put that on the shelf, so to speak. Another thing He told me during that time was that I would one day minister to women. I *sure* didn't want to do that! So I put that on the shelf too.

Then He said, "And you'll be teaching and ministering both to men and women." I trembled at that. I said,

"Lord, You must be mistaken! You've got the wrong person in mind. I'm good at teaching children, not adults."

Finally He told me something that I actually *wanted* to do. He said my husband and I would one day minister to ministers. I thought, *Thank You, God. I'm glad You finally gave me something that I want to do!*

Well, by that time, I had already *committed* to doing the will of God and had proved it by moving from Dallas to Tulsa. So I was ready to get started actually *doing* the will of God! I said, "Okay, God, I'm ready to do what You've told me to do. Let's get busy!"

I got busy all right—busy *waiting!* Years passed, and I was still waiting. But not just waiting, praying—waiting for His timing and praying for His instructions on how to go about fulfilling the plan He had given me. Now I had a list, and there was so much to do—lead others in prayer, hold women's conferences, teach men and women, and minister to ministers.

As you know, when it finally came time to get busy, the first thing God asked me to do wasn't even on the list! It was choosing wallpaper, carpet, and paint. My husband was in charge of building the RHEMA campus, and he asked me to decorate the buildings.

Hey, God, Why Is It Taking So Long?

I was so happy just to be out of the house doing something for the Lord that I agreed to do it. I had no experience and didn't know what I was getting myself into. The job grew bigger and bigger! It quickly got to the point where it was beyond my qualifications.

So I complained to the Lord, "God, why did You call me to do this? I don't even want to do this. I don't like it. I don't feel qualified to do it."

I had forgotten that I had been asking Him for something to do in the ministry, telling Him I was willing to do *anything at all*. I started complaining to Him a lot and telling Him what tasks He *should* assign me, telling Him what I *wanted* to do. I said, "This place needs to be organized. I'm a good drill sergeant. I can get all these offices and departments organized. I can write out all of their procedures. I can do that really well, Lord."

I thought the Lord would be proud of me because I wanted to do something for Him that I could do really well. I was communing with Him, saying, "Lord, I know You want me to do what I can do really well," when He spoke something to me that I will never forget.

In almost an audible voice, the Lord said sternly, "Lynette, that's the problem! You want to do everything that you can do relying on your own ability. But then you don't have to have any faith in Me. You don't have to trust Me. You don't have to have any confidence in Me, because you can do it in your own natural ability."

Someone could have physically knocked me down and it would have felt better! Then He said something else to me that I will never forget, "Lynette, there's no way you can accomplish in your strength, knowledge, and ability what I have ultimately called you to do. You have no option but to learn to trust Me. You must learn to lean on My strength and ability. I'm teaching you through this simple task of decorating how to rely on Me and on My strength and ability."

I knew then and there that it would be a supernatural decorating job. And, oh, the things I learned! I learned to rely on God and to trust in Him as He worked through me according to His plan and purpose. I learned to lean on the Lord Jesus Christ and to wait on Him while He did a work in me. I learned to rest and relax in Him and to stop worrying about the future.

Rest in the Lord

I learned to say, "Okay, God, I'm going to hold Your hand. I'm not going to think about tomorrow. I'm not going to try to figure everything out. But I'm going to hold on to Your hand and not rely on my ability for anything.

295

Whatever You want me to do each day is what we're going to do. And I won't worry about what You told me is going to happen in the future."

So many times we get our eyes on the end result—focusing on the faraway future—and forget about the waiting process that must take place in the meantime. The following is part of a prophetic utterance I received from the Lord as I ministered in a church service.

The waiting process is far longer than you imagined.

But rest in Me, rely on Me.

Yes, you've been faithful.

But continue to be patient; continue to be patient!

For just in the near future, the plan shall unfold to you very quickly.

Very clearly! Very clearly!

So don't give up. Don't be in unrest.

Don't move out of My will. . . .

Don't move until you know.

That cloud has so engulfed you that you haven't even been able to think clearly.

You've lost your joy.

Now break through that. Break through that! Break through that!

You know how to do it! Yes, you know how to do it.

And as you break through that, such sunshine is just around the corner.

But there's a spiritual battle going on,

And because of your zeal, you want to press on in the wrong area. . . .

Get back to [hearing] *My voice, and I'll speak that to you again.*

You've got it a little bit wrong, but this time as I speak it to you,

It will be so clear. It'll be so clear!

And the anointing that shall accompany it will be powerful.

And it will touch many lives. . . in time.

Make the choice to wait upon the Lord. When you make that choice, things will come around, but you must first make that choice. You keep praying, "Lord, show me the road ahead." But you've got it backwards. He can't show you the road ahead until you make that choice.

When you trust in the Lord with all your heart, He will lead and guide you along a good path for your life.

Hey, God, Why Is It Taking So Long?

Regardless of your past, when you wait upon the Lord and trust in Him, everything will be all right. The devil may have thought he had you beat, but don't quit! Don't give up! Keep fighting until you win, and everything will turn out all right!

Some day soon, the things of earth will indeed grow dim. They won't even matter to us anymore, because we're going to be walking on the glory clouds with our Lord Jesus. We gladly look for that great day when the Heavenly Father looks over and says, "Son, go bring My children home." What a joyous and glorious time that will be! But right now is our time. It's your time. The Lord is saying, "Take your place. Move up to that higher plane." It's a plane you've not seen before. You may have seen parts of it; you may have stepped on the edge of it, but now it's time to live on it!

Build yourself up; prepare yourself for your calling—to march forward in the ways of the Lord, lifting His banner high! And as you do, you will walk out your calling, complete God's mission, and fulfill your purpose. Then the Lord will say to you, "Well done, thou good and faithful servant."

I'm excited about what God has in store for us when we wait upon Him. As you do, when the enemy starts telling you that you're missing it, when he tries to get you off course by telling you time is running out, just tell him what the Word says! "They that wait upon the Lord shall renew their strength. They shall mount up with wings as eagles; they shall run and not be weary; they shall walk and not faint! [Isa. 40:31]"

Personal Prayer:

Father, to do Your will is my greatest desire. I choose to wait on You. I wait for clear vision and clear direction concerning Your plan for my life. Father, thank You for speaking very clearly, speak very strongly, and reveal Your plan to me by Your Holy Spirit. I will wait upon You and trust You to tell me what to do and when and how to do it. Father, right now I dedicate and consecrate myself to following Your path. From this day forward, I will rest in You as I fulfill Your purpose for my life. In Jesus' Name, I pray. Amen.

---

[1] David Ingles, "My Confidence Is Great (in the Lord)," © 1991 David Ingles Music.

CHAPTER 15

For Such a Time as This

We live in a busy, busy world—*too* busy sometimes. We expect so much of ourselves. For us to keep up, it seems we always have to be learning more and doing more. We not only expect a lot from ourselves and from our family, but we also expect a lot from other people. We even expect a lot from God. We keep Him very busy tending to all of our requests. Can you imagine all the requests God must hear in one day's time? "God, please do this." "God, please do that." "God, help me." But, thank the Lord, He is able to attend to all of us.

Sometimes life is so busy that I feel like I'm in a whirlwind and I'm barely holding on. Have you ever felt that way? Have you ever felt as if you were no longer in control of your life?

Hey, God, Why Is It Taking So Long?

Many times, we become frustrated because what we expected to happen did not happen. We become disappointed. We become disappointed in others—in our children or family, or in ourselves. There are times we even become disappointed in God. We think, *God, why didn't You come through for me this time?* Other people may indeed let you down, and you may even let yourself down. But God comes through every time. It just may not be how you thought He would come through.

Every pain, every frustration, every offense, every hurt you experienced in the past was the result of a failed expectation. In other words, something that you expected to happen either did not happen the way you wanted it to, or it did not happen at all. Perhaps you had a need and expected someone to meet that need, but that person failed you. Maybe you wanted to take some time off work and thought your boss would let you, but he didn't. Perhaps you asked your spouse to do something, and they let you down. When those people disappointed you, you may have felt as though you didn't have control of your life. Those feelings of disappointment or lack of control can lead to deeper hurts, frustration, and even anger.

Sometimes we think that if we can just gain control of our life, we would have it made. If we could just organize our life, we would have it made. And we are admonished over and over again to take charge of our life to the point that we may feel guilty when we feel we don't measure up. We feel condemned when we haven't taken charge of our life to the degree that people or books or so-called experts tell us to.

So what do we do then? We buy a daily planner and start trying to organize and schedule our life, hoping that doing so will make us feel more in control. We read time management books, hoping they will help us accomplish more so we feel we are taking charge of our life. We go to seminars and think the instructors have everything under control. They lecture us and we think, *If only I could be in control of life the way they are.* But they probably don't have any more control in life than we do.

We think that if we could be in control of our life, we would feel better about ourselves. Control can be a very big issue for all of us—and I'm no exception. In fact, control used to be a *very big* issue for me.

Learning to Yield Control

By nature, I'm a very organized person. I'm also a perfectionist. From very early on, I wanted my life to be planned out from A to Z. As I've said, I wanted to know every detail of what I would be doing in 5 years, 10 years, and even 20 years. Knowing the future and planning ahead was very important to me and became a very big issue in my life.

When it came to serving God, I knew I wanted to commit my life to the Lord. I knew I was called to work in the ministry, but I wanted God to show me the 20-year plan before I had to truly commit to anything. I prided myself in having charge of my life. But that was the key: I, not *God*, was in charge of my life.

Jeremiah 29:11 says, "'For I know the plans that I have for you,' declares the Lord, 'plans for welfare and not for calamity to give you a future and a hope'" (*NASB*). God is the speaker in this verse. He is the One saying, "I know the plans I have for you." Notice that God has His own plans for us. They are His plans, not our plans. One of the hardest things to do is to commit to following God's plan instead of our own.

Even when I say "I commit to following God's plan," my natural tendency is to try to help God out. I'm a very organized person—surely I can help God with the organization! But, of course, God does not need any help planning my life. In fact, *He* wants to plan my life for me—without my help! The best thing I can do to help God is to get out of His way.

That's not an easy task, because we think that we can live life on our own—at least some aspects of it. But when the Lord plans our path, or orders our steps, then even if we fall, the Lord is there to hold us up.

PSALM 37:23–25

23 The steps of a good man are ordered by the Lord: and he delighteth in his way. 24 Though he fall, he shall not be utterly cast down: for the Lord upholdeth him with his hand.

25 I have been young, and now am old; yet have I not seen the righteous forsaken, nor his seed begging bread.

If we will let the Lord guide our steps, He will lead us down the right path. And as He leads us down the right path, we will not be begging for bread—we won't be in want. The Lord will show us the right way to go, even if it's not the path we think we should take.

Many times we don't want to follow the path God has for us. We want to get from Point A to Point B on the shortest, quickest, straightest, easiest path possible. But life doesn't always take a straight path; we can't always go from A to B in one straight line. It would be great if we could, but more often than not, we go this way, that way, and the other way before we reach our destination! But if it's the path the Lord has marked for us, then it is the best path we could ever possibly take.

I remember a minister who gave me a Bible when I was just a teenager, and in it, he wrote the scripture reference Proverbs 3:5–6. This passage became a very important part of my life, helping me trust in the Lord and in His plan for my life when I wanted to make my own plans.

God has a specific plan for your life, *and* He has a specific timeline for each part of that plan to unfold. It's so important to let the Lord direct your path according to His timing, because the right plan acted upon at the wrong time can become a disaster. So it's important that each one of us say, "Okay, Lord, I may not understand the path You are leading me on, but I'm going to accept that path. And I'm going to walk in that path in peace, knowing that the end result will be for my good. I know that You have a plan for my life that includes a future and a hope."

Esther Fulfills Her Destiny

What if the great men and women of the Bible had not followed God wholeheartedly? What if they had not walked in the right steps at the right time?

You may have already read the story of Esther from the Book of Esther in the Bible. I like her story very much and I want to share parts of it with you, because I believe it will help us see that we, too, have a divine purpose on this earth. And we, too, have been called into the Kingdom *for such a time as this*.

I want to begin the story with the king's decree that all the Jews be killed. Esther, although she was queen, was herself Jewish, and was to be killed with the rest of her people. Her uncle Mordecai calls upon her to do something to save her people.

ESTHER 3:2,5–6,8–10; 4:1–5,7–14

2   And all the king's servants, that were in the king's gate, bowed, and reverenced Haman: for the king had so commanded concerning him. But Mordecai bowed not, nor did him reverence. . . .

5   And when Haman saw that Mordecai bowed not, nor did him reverence, then was Haman full of wrath.

6   And he thought scorn to lay hands on Mordecai alone; for they had shewed him the people of Mordecai: wherefore Haman sought to destroy all the Jews that were throughout

the whole kingdom of Ahasuerus, even the people of Mordecai. . . .

8 And Haman said unto king Ahasuerus, There is a certain people scattered abroad and dispersed among the people in all the provinces of thy kingdom; and their laws are diverse from all people; neither keep they the king's laws: therefore it is not for the king's profit to suffer them.

9 If it please the king, let it be written that they may be destroyed: and I will pay ten thousand talents of silver to the hands of those that have the charge of the business, to bring it into the king's treasuries.

10 And the king took his ring from his hand, and gave it unto Haman the son of Hammedatha the Agagite, the Jews' enemy. . . .

1 When Mordecai perceived all that was done, Mordecai rent his clothes, and put on sackcloth with ashes, and went out into the midst of the city, and cried with a loud and a bitter cry;

2 And came even before the king's gate: THIS none might enter into the king's gate clothed with sackcloth.

3 And in every province, whithersoever the king's commandment and his decree came, there was great mourning among the Jews, and fasting, and weeping, and wailing; and many lay in sackcloth and ashes.

4 So Esther's maids and her chamberlains came and told it her. Then was the queen exceedingly grieved; and she sent raiment to clothe Mordecai, and to take away his sackcloth from him: but he received it not.

5 Then called Esther for Hatach, one of the king's chamberlains, whom he had appointed to attend upon her, and gave him a commandment to Mordecai, to know what it was, and why it was. . . .

7 And Mordecai told him of all that had happened unto him, and of the sum of the money that Haman had promised to pay to the king's treasuries for the Jews, to destroy them.

8 Also he gave him the copy of the writing of the decree that was given at Shushan to destroy them, to shew it unto Esther, and to declare it unto her, and to charge her that she should go in unto the king, to make supplication unto him, and to make request before him for her people.

9 And Hatach came and told Esther the words of Mordecai.

10 Again Esther spake unto Hatach, and gave him commandment unto Mordecai;

11 All the king's servants, and the people of the king's provinces, do know, that whosoever, whether man or women, shall come unto the king into the inner court, who is not called, there is one law of his to put him to death, except such to whom the king shall hold out the golden sceptre, that he may live: but I have not been called to come in unto the king these thirty days.

12 And they told to Mordecai Esther's words.

13 Then Mordecai commanded to answer Esther, Think not with thyself that thou shalt

escape in the king's house, more than all the Jews.

14 For if thou altogether holdest thy peace at this time, then shall there enlargement and deliverance arise to the Jews from another place; but thou and thy father's house shall be destroyed: and who knoweth whether thou ART COME TO THE KINGDOM FOR SUCH A TIME AS THIS?

Haman, the king's highest-ranking official, had talked the king into sending out a decree for all the Jews to be killed. But the king didn't know that his queen was Jewish. Mordecai sent word to Esther, "Don't think that you will be spared just because you are the queen. If all of the Jews are to be killed, you're going to be killed too." Then he said these great words in Esther 4:14, *"For if thou altogether holdest thy peace at this time, then shall there enlargement and deliverance arise to the Jews from another place; but thou and thy father's house shall be destroyed: and who knoweth whether thou art come to the kingdom for such a time as this?"*

What did Esther decide to do? She chose to fulfill her God-given destiny, to save her people, and to walk the path God had marked for her—even if it meant her death.

Hey, God, Why Is It Taking So Long?

ESTHER 4:15–17

15 Then Esther bade them return Mordecai this answer,

16 Go, gather together all the Jews that are present in Shushan, and fast ye for me, and neither eat nor drink three days, night or day: I also and my maidens will fast likewise; and so will I go in unto the king, which is not according to the law: and if I perish, I perish.

17 So Mordecai went his way, and did according to all that Esther had commanded him.

Esther came into her natural kingdom in order to fulfill the plan of God for her life and in order to save her people. And *you* have come to God's Kingdom for such a time as this! It is going to take many people to accomplish what God has called His people to do. And one of those people is *you*.

You have a special place in God's great plan. Don't try to take someone else's place. Esther may have wished she could have taken someone else's place. I doubt she wanted to approach the king without being summoned and thereby risk being put to death. But she found her place and filled it.

Many of us at one time or another have wished we had received someone else's calling. We've probably all asked at one time or another, "God, why couldn't You call me to do such-and-such?"

I hear ministers say, "Why can't I just be a successful businessman? Then I wouldn't have to deal with all of these people's problems every day." And I hear people in business say, "Why can't I be in the ministry? I would love to stand up and preach every week." But God has a plan and purpose and destiny for each and every one of us. You have been chosen to carry out the purpose that He has for your life. And it's so important that you find that purpose and fulfill it.

You may say, "Lynette, I know what you're saying is right, but I've been on this earth for 40 years, and I still don't know my purpose in life." If you don't know God's purpose for your life, get down on your knees and say, "God, I'm not going to let You go until you tell me why I'm here and what my purpose is in life."

You *do* have a purpose. God created and formed you to be different from any other person. After He made you, He threw away the mold! You are one of a kind.

Again, Psalm 139:14 says, *"I will praise thee; for I am fearfully and wonderfully made: marvellous are thy works; and that my soul knoweth right well."* It's time for you to start praising God for the way He made you, because He made you wonderfully well. You have talents that God has given you. It's time to quit concentrating on the negative things in your life, because when you focus on the negative things, they become so big that all you can see is what you are not. *Stop looking at what you are not and start looking at what you are!*

You Can Do All Things Through Christ

If you have trouble believing these positive things I'm saying about you, find scriptures that say the same thing and continue to read them, quote them, and hold on to them. Second Corinthians 5:21 says you are the righteousness of God in Christ. Philippians 4:13 says you can do all things through Christ who strengthens you.

God rarely calls us to a place where we can be comfortable in our own talents and abilities. He wants to move us out of our comfort zones. He wants us to depend upon Him—and we will have to if we are to accomplish all that He has planned for our life.

If you are having a problem trusting God's plan—if you have reached a point in your life where it seems you can't make it to the other side—take the hand of the Lord and literally quote Philippians 4:13 every day. On a daily basis say aloud, "I can do all things through Christ who strengthens me." This will help remind you that you have God's help in fulfilling His plan and you don't have to live life on your own. If you need wisdom to know how to walk out God's plan, daily quote James 1:5, which says, *"If any of you lack wisdom, let him ask of God, that giveth to all men liberally, and upbraideth not; and it shall be given him."* Remind yourself on a daily basis that God's wisdom belongs to you! *You have His wisdom and His strength to fulfill His purpose for your life!*

To be honest, sometimes walking in God's plan has been scary for me and sometimes it's *still* scary for me. But now when I feel frightened that the plan is just too much for me, I close my eyes, so to speak, and trust God to take me to the other side. Each and every day I say, "Father, I can't do what You've called me to in my own strength. But I know that in Your strength and in Your ability, I can do all things."

Rewards for Faithfulness

Maybe you have been called to be successful in business. Perhaps you have been called to be a lawyer, artist, manager, secretary, singer, teacher, or salesperson. Maybe you have been called to help your pastor fulfill the vision that God has placed on his heart. Whatever your calling may be, never belittle what you have been called to do.

When the rewards are handed out in Heaven, they will not be based on how much you have done or how great your accomplishments were. The rewards are given according to faithfulness. How faithful were you to God's call on your life? How faithful were you in following His plan for you?

When we get to Heaven and are lined up to receive our rewards, there may be many people whom we've considered great in God's Kingdom whose rewards will be less than those of the "unknown" person who faithfully followed God's plan for his or her life. God hasn't called all of us to do the same thing. All He asks is that we be faithful in what He *has* called us to do.

Queen Esther's steps were ordered of the Lord. What might have happened to her if she had gone to see the king at the wrong time? What might have happened if Esther had said the wrong thing when she approached the king? The plan, or what we do, is important—*when* we do it and *how* we do it are also important. It's so important that we stay sensitive to the Lord and learn to follow His every step as He leads us and guides us.

Moses Followed God's Plan

Along with Esther, Moses is someone else I admire for the courageous way he followed God's plan for his life.

Moses had a special calling and was protected by God even from his birth. He was born during a time when Pharaoh had declared that every male Israelite baby be killed. Midwives were instructed to allow baby girls to live but to kill baby boys. What would have happened if the midwives delivering Moses had not feared and obeyed God? What would have happened if they had not been following the plan of God, but were following Pharaoh's plan instead?

EXODUS 2:1–15 (*NIV*)

1   Now a man of the house of Levi married a Levite woman,

2   and she became pregnant and gave birth to a son. When she saw that he was a fine child, she hid him for three months.

3   But when she could hide him no longer, she got a papyrus basket for him and coated it with tar and pitch. Then she placed the child in it and put it among the reeds along the bank of the Nile.

4   His sister stood at a distance to see what would happen to him.

5   When Pharaoh's daughter went down to the Nile to bathe, and her attendants were walking along the river bank. She saw the basket among the reeds and sent her slave girl to get it.

6   She opened it and saw the baby. He was crying, and she felt sorry for him. "This is one of the Hebrew babies," she said.

7   Then his sister asked Pharaoh's daughter, "Shall I go and get one of the Hebrew women to nurse the baby for you?"

8   "Yes, go," she answered. And the girl went and got the baby's mother.

9 Pharaoh's daughter said to her, "Take this baby and nurse him for me, and I will pay you." So the woman took the baby and nursed him.

10 When the child grew older, she took him to Pharaoh's daughter and he became her son. She named him Moses, saying, "I drew him out of the water."

11 One day, after Moses had grown up, he went out to where his own people were and watched them at their hard labor. He saw an Egyptian beating a Hebrew, one of his own people.

12 Glancing this way and that and seeing no-one, he killed the Egyptian and hid him in the sand.

13 The next day he went out and saw two Hebrews fighting. He asked the one in the wrong, "Why are you hitting your fellow Hebrew?"

14 The man said, "Who made you ruler and judge over us? Are you thinking of killing me as you killed the Egyptian?" Then Moses was afraid and thought, "What I did must have become known."

15 When Pharaoh heard of this, he tried to kill Moses, but Moses fled from Pharaoh and went to live in Midian, where he sat down by a well.

God's plan for Moses' life could not be thwarted by Pharaoh's evil decree. Moses was saved at birth and placed in reeds along the Nile River. Pharaoh's daughter found him and rescued him, so Moses was raised as her son in Pharaoh's palace! I'm sure he was happy there. Wouldn't you be happy if you were raised as the Pharaoh's grandchild instead of living as a captive slave?

One day when he was an adult, Moses became angry when he saw an Egyptian hitting a Hebrew slave. Moses was so angry that he killed the Egyptian. Then Moses became afraid that Pharaoh would find out what he had done, so he ran and hid.

You may have done something in the past that you're ashamed of and have been "hiding" from God. It's time to run *to* God, ask His forgiveness, and move ahead with His plan for your life.

It's important that we not let fear dominate our life, because fear can cause us to miss out on God's plan for our life. Don't be afraid, saying, "God, I can't do it." Yes, you *can*!

One of the things my dad told me and I've kept as a philosophy in life is this: "The phrase 'It can't be done' should not exist in our vocabulary." The old saying is true, *Where there is a will, there is a way*. Never say something can't be done, because with God, we can do anything He's asked us to do.

Fear began to dominate Moses' life, and the very thing he greatly feared came upon him—Pharaoh discovered what he had done. The Bible tells us that Moses fled to Midian where he became a shepherd.

EXODUS 2:16–25 (*NIV*)

16 Now a priest of Midian had seven daughters, and they came to draw water and fill the troughs to water their father's flock.

17 Some shepherds came along and drove them away, but Moses got up and came to their rescue and watered their flock.

18 When the girls returned to Reuel their father, he asked them, "Why have you returned so early today?"

19 They answered, "An Egyptian rescued us from the shepherds. He even drew water for us and watered the flock."

20 "And where is he?" he asked his daughters. "Why did you leave him? Invite him to have something to eat."

21 Moses agreed to stay with the man, who gave his daughter Zipporah to Moses in marriage.

22 Zipporah gave birth to a son, and Moses named him Gershom, saying, "I have become an alien in a foreign land."

23 During that long period, the king of Egypt died. The Israelites groaned in their slavery and cried out, and their cry for help because of their slavery went up to God.

24 God heard their groaning and he remembered his covenant with Abraham, with Isaac and with Jacob.

25 So God looked on the Israelites and was concerned about them.

Moses got married and went about his life, working as a shepherd. He may have figured that was all he would ever do. But in the meantime, the children of Israel grew tired of being slaves and cried out to God for deliverance. And God heard their prayers!

I've often wondered if the Israelites would have been delivered sooner had they just *asked* sooner. You see, God's Word says that we have not because we ask not (James 4:2). It is so important that we ask.

If you want something from God, ask Him. Our Heavenly Father delights in answering the requests of *all* His children.

If you're a parent, don't you love to please your children? Don't you love to see the smile on their face when you're able to give them something they've wanted and asked for? Maybe they wanted a bicycle and you were able to give them one—their grateful and happy smile is worth a million dollars.

Our Heavenly Father loves to give good gifts to His children even more than we natural parents love giving gifts to ours! Matthew 7:11 says, *"If you, then, though you are evil* [or natural], *know how to give good gifts to your children, how much more will your Father in heaven give good gifts to those who ASK him!"*

Notice that we must ask our Heavenly Father for that which we desire. John 16:24 says, *"Hitherto have ye asked nothing in my name: ASK, and ye shall receive, that your joy may be full."* What do you have need of? Ask your Heavenly Father for it, believing that you receive it, and you shall have it (Mark. 11:24).

God Chose Moses as the Deliverer

The children of Israel asked God to deliver them, and God chose Moses to be the deliverer.

Moses had lived in a strange land for 40 years. He might have felt as though God had forgotten him. Maybe he felt that he had messed up the great life he could have had in Pharaoh's palace. Perhaps the guilt from his past mistakes made him think he was useless to God. But God knew exactly where Moses was and what he was doing.

In fact, God had been watching Moses all along—as he ran from Egypt and Pharaoh, as he married, and as he

323

tended flocks. God knew the plan He had for Moses, and His plan remained, even when Moses was seemingly following his own path.

EXODUS 3:1–15 (*NIV*)

1   Now Moses was tending the flock of Jethro his father-in-law, the priest of Midian, and he led the flock to the far side of the desert and came to Horeb, the mountain of God.

2   There the angel of the Lord appeared to him in flames of fire from within a bush. Moses saw that though the bush was on fire it did not burn up.

3   So Moses thought, "I will go over and see this strange sight—why the bush does not burn up."

4   When the Lord saw that he had gone over to look, God called to him from within the bush, "Moses! Moses!" And Moses said, "Here I am."

5   "Do not come any closer," God said. "Take off your sandals, for the place where you are standing is holy ground."

6 Then he said, "I am the God of your father, the God of Abraham, the God of Isaac and the God of Jacob." At this, Moses hid his face, because he was afraid to look at God.

7 The Lord said, "I have indeed seen the misery of my people in Egypt. I have heard them crying out because of their slave drivers, and I am concerned about their suffering.

8 So I have come down to rescue them from the hand of the Egyptians and to bring them up out of that land into a good and spacious land, a land flowing with milk and honey— the home of the Canaanites, Hittites, Amorites, Perizzites, Hivites and Jebusites.

9 And now the cry of the Israelites has reached me, and I have seen the way the Egyptians are oppressing them.

10 So now, go. I am sending you to Pharaoh to bring my people the Israelites out of Egypt."

11 But Moses said to God, "Who am I, that I should go to Pharaoh and bring the Israelites out of Egypt?"

12 And God said, "I will be with you. And this will be the sign to you that it is I who have sent you: When you have brought the people out of Egypt, you will worship God on this mountain."

13 Moses said to God, "Suppose I go to the Israelites and say to them, 'The God of your fathers has sent me to you,' and they ask me, 'What is his name?' Then what shall I tell them?"

14 God said to Moses, "I AM WHO I AM. This is what you are to say to the Israelites: 'I AM has sent me to you.'"

15 God also said to Moses, "Say to the Israelites, 'The Lord, the God of your fathers—the God of Abraham, the God of Isaac and the God of Jacob—has sent me to you.' This is my name forever, the name by which I am to be remembered from generation to generation."

Moses was 40 years old when he escaped to Midian. There he lived as a shepherd for 40 more years—just minding his own business and tending his sheep. Suddenly, God appeared to him. Mind you, Moses was now 80 years old.

When people pass 80 nowadays, we think they are pretty much finished with the big events of life. But Moses was 80 and *just beginning* to do what God had called him to do.

I can just imagine God standing up from His Throne, looking down, and saying to Moses, "Moses, you were called for such a time as this. This is why you were born— for such a time as this."

When Moses saw that the fire did not consume the bush, he recognized that a supernatural event was taking place. It's so important in our life to be able to recognize when something supernatural is happening. We should never be so busy with the affairs of life that we are not attentively attuned to the voice of God. We must strive to always keep our spiritual eyes and ears open.

It's real easy to get ahead of what God wants you to do. As Brother Hagin often said, "I'd rather be two steps behind God than one step in front of Him." It's very important that we continually listen to God and allow Him to direct our every step.

God proceeded to assign Moses the task that He had called him to do and that was to lead the children of Israel out of Egypt. Now Moses could have had the attitude "Why should I help *them*? I had to leave the easy life and flee because of them, so why should I risk my life now to lead them out?" But Moses had been preserved for that very hour.

Of course, Moses was also a little scared—daunted by the great task before him—and wondered, *Who am I to do this?* So Moses had an argument with God, trying to convince God that he wasn't qualified for the job. He told God that he didn't speak well and kept arguing his case.

Sometimes when we are still in our spiritual infancy, God in His mercy will give us a supernatural sign when He asks us to do something. But as we grow and mature as Christians, He expects us to learn to listen to His voice and to follow the leading of His Spirit. There may be times when you are first learning to hear His voice that He will speak to you in more tangible or audible ways. But as you grow spiritually, He expects you to become sensitive to His voice, and at that point, you shouldn't need a sign to know that you heard from God.

Moses asked God, "What am I to say to the children of Israel when I tell them that I'm to lead them out of Egypt? Where is my authority coming from? Whom shall I say sent me?" And God told Moses exactly what to say.

EXODUS 3:13–14

13 And Moses said unto God, Behold, when I come unto the children of Israel, and shall say

unto them, The God of your fathers hath sent me unto you; and they shall say to me, What is his name? what shall I say unto them?

14 And God said unto Moses, I AM THAT I AM: and he said, Thus shalt thou say unto the children of Israel, I AM hath sent me unto you.

Did you know that *I AM* has sent *you* to accomplish what He has called you to do? The Great I AM has sent you. You are qualified. You will be a success in life if you wholly follow the Lord.

Caleb Possesses His Mountain

When it comes to wholly following God's plan in life, I'm reminded of another person in the Bible whom I admire very much—Caleb. Caleb was faithful to follow God's plan for His life. He believed the words God spoke concerning the future, even when the rest of the Israelites didn't. And he was faithful to obey God wholeheartedly, no matter what anyone else did.

In Numbers chapter 13, we read that Moses sent twelve spies to explore the land of Canaan. Ten spies came back saying, "We should turn back. There are giants in the land. We were like grasshoppers in our own eyes and in theirs" (vv. 31–33). Caleb's report was different. Numbers 13:30 says, *"And Caleb stilled the people before Moses, and said, Let us go up at once, and possess it; for we are well able to overcome it."* You know the story: the Israelites did not go up to take their Promised Land but wandered in the wilderness for the next 40 years.

After the death of Moses, Joshua became the leader of the Israelites. Caleb could have gotten jealous because Joshua had been chosen to lead the children of Israel rather than him. Caleb was with Joshua when they and 10 others spied out the Promised Land. Caleb came back with just as good a report as Joshua did. Caleb could easily have been jealous of Joshua. And if this had happened in our day, many Christians would have lost their blessing and would have missed God because they would have been jealous. They would have complained, "Why is So-and-so being used instead of me? I'm just as qualified as he is. I've been more faithful than he's been." But Caleb didn't get jealous. The Word says he followed God wholeheartedly. He kept his eye on what God had promised him and kept following in God's steps.

JOSHUA 14:6–12 (*NIV*)

6 Now the men of Judah approached Joshua at Gilgal, and Caleb son of Jephunneh the

Kenizzite said to him, "You know what the
Lord said to Moses the man of God at Kadesh
Barnea about you and me.

7   I was forty years old when Moses the servant of the Lord sent me from Kadesh Barnea
to explore the land. And I brought him back a
report according to my convictions,

8   but my brothers who went up with me
made the hearts of the people melt with fear.
I, HOWEVER, FOLLOWED THE LORD MY
GOD WHOLEHEARTEDLY.

9   So on that day Moses swore to me, 'The
land on which your feet have walked will be
your inheritance and that of your children
forever, BECAUSE YOU HAVE FOLLOWED
THE LORD MY GOD WHOLEHEARTEDLY.'

10 "Now then, just as the Lord promised, he
has kept me alive for forty-five years since the
time he said this to Moses, while Israel moved
about in the desert. So here I am today,
eighty-five years old!

11 I AM STILL AS STRONG TODAY AS
THE DAY MOSES SENT ME OUT; I'M JUST

AS VIGOROUS TO GO OUT TO BATTLE NOW AS I WAS THEN.

12 Now give me this hill country that the Lord promised me that day. You yourself heard then that the Anakites were there and their cities were large and fortified, but, THE LORD HELPING ME, I WILL DRIVE THEM OUT JUST AS HE SAID."

There Caleb was—85 years old and ready to take the mountain God has promised him when he was 40! What would we say in today's society to an 85-year-old man who had plans to do great things for God? We might say, "Well, you're too old to be used of God." Or, "You're too feeble and don't have enough energy to do great things. Let the young people take over . . ."

The Word says that as a man thinks in his heart so is he (Prov. 23:7). If you think you're "old," you will be old. But if you think "young," you'll look, feel, and act young. If you are naturally young in years right now, you may think you don't need to hear this. One day you will!

As you get older, you have to talk to your body as the great preacher Smith Wigglesworth did. You have to tell your body what to do and how it's going to feel. My body doesn't tell *me* what to do; *I* tell *my body* what to do. I'm known for walking super fast. People always think I'm in a hurry, but it's the pace at which I walk all the time.

One day while I was on the road with my husband holding a healing crusade, I was walking and talking with our crusade manager. He was 30 at the time, and I was almost 53, and he had to hustle to keep up with me! I told the manager, "You know what? When you're 73 and I'm 95, you're *still* going to be trying to keep up with me! I tell my body what to do, and I tell it do it *fast*!"

I have two speeds—fast and not at all. If I'm awake, I'm always going fast. The only time my speed is different is when I'm asleep! It's going to take getting into high gear to accomplish all that the Lord has for us to do!

You may have been sitting on the back burner, so to speak, thinking that life has passed you by. Maybe you haven't accomplished what you thought God had for your life, and you think your chance is gone. You need to say, "I'm just as strong today as I was when I was 20 [or 30 or 40 or 50]."

Caleb didn't deny natural facts. In the natural, circumstances were against him. There were enemies inhabiting the land that God had promised him, and Caleb was getting older! Caleb admitted that the cities were large and fortified and inhabited by enemies. *And* he admitted his age.

Hey, God, Why Is It Taking So Long?

But what else did Caleb say? He said, *"I am still as strong today as the day Moses sent me out; I'm just as vigorous to go out to battle now as I was then. Now give me this hill country that the Lord promised me that day. You yourself heard then that the Anakites were there and their cities were large and fortified, but, the Lord helping me, I will drive them out just as he said"* (vv. 11,12).

Caleb recognized the facts, but he was armed with the greater facts of God's Word. He knew God was on his side, and with God he would win!

The facts may be that you are being attacked. But the greater fact is that the Lord is on your side, helping you. If God be for you, who can be against you? You will drive out the enemy just as He said!

God Has Not Forgotten You

I want to encourage you to remind yourself of God's call on your life. If that call once burned bright in your heart but has now dimmed, remind yourself of what God spoke to your heart in the beginning. Build yourself up on His promises because they fail not! Even if He called you long ago, and you have allowed many years to go by without fulfilling His plan, don't despair. It's never too late to start following God's plan for your life. You may need to tell yourself, "I'm just as vigorous and just as strong as I was when I was 20! And with the Lord helping me, I *can* and *will* do what He has called me to do!"

And if the devil tries to tell you that it's too late or that you're unfit, you tell him in no uncertain terms, "Devil! I will not allow you to get me off course or keep me off course. I will not allow you to distract me. I will not allow you to tempt me. I will not allow you to discourage me. My God is with me. I AM THAT I AM has sent me. I may have deficiencies in myself, but I am all sufficient in the Lord.

"I will not allow you, devil, to rob me of my health, because my body is being quickened, my body is being strengthened. I will not allow you to rob me of my strength. I will not allow you to rob me of my finances. I will not allow you to dominate me, for I am here to declare before you and all your cohorts that I AM THAT I AM has sent me.

"I will be a success in life. I will fulfill my destiny. And when I stand before the Lord in Heaven, He will say to me, 'Well done, My good and faithful servant. You have been faithful over a few things, and I will make you ruler over many.'"

God has a plan for your life! At every twist and turn in the road of life, God has known right where you were and He has never changed His mind about His love for you or His plan for your life. Even if you allowed yourself to get off course—whether you became distracted by other things, missed it and sinned, or just plain refused to do the will of God—God wants to get you back on the path of His choosing. And you can do it if you will just answer His call, and follow His plan—one step at a time!

Are you ready to fulfill that which God has called you to do? Are you ready to live the plan He has designed just for you? You will be a success as you fulfill God's destiny for your life, take each step, and do what He has called you to do. You shall be invigorated with God's power, energy, and strength. And you shall take your place in the earth for such a time as this.

About the Author

Passionate, prayerful, prophetic. These words describe the ministry of Lynette Hagin. Spurring believers everywhere to step up higher spiritually, Lynette is a leader in declaring the greater move of God in this last day.

Lynette serves as director of RHEMA Bible Training Center and general manager of Kenneth Hagin Ministries, and assists her husband, Rev. Kenneth Hagin Jr., in pastoring RHEMA Bible Church.

Her leadership in ministry has been instrumental in shaping the lives of thousands of women through her annual *Kindle the Flame* Women's Conference. And many more lives are touched through *RHEMA Praise*, a weekly television broadcast Lynette co-hosts with her husband.

Lynette and her husband, Ken, have been married since 1965. They have two grown children and five grandsons.

God has a *specific* plan for your life.
Are you ready?
RHEMA Bible Training Center

∞ Take your place in the Body of Christ for the last great revival.

∞ Learn to rightly divide God's Word and to hear His voice clearly.

∞ Discover how to be a willing vessel for God's glory.

∞ Receive practical hands-on ministry training from experienced
ministers.

*Qualified instructors are waiting to teach, train,
and help **you** fulfill your destiny!*

Call today for information or application material.
1-888-28-FAITH (1-888-283-2484)—Offer #4450

www.rbtc.org

RHEMA Bible Training Center admits students of any race, color, or ethnic origin.